The ART *and*
PRACTICE
of
COMPASSION
&
EMPATHY

The ART and PRACTICE of COMPASSION & EMPATHY

Margot Lasher, Ph.D.

A Jeremy P. Tarcher/Putnam Book
published by
G. P. PUTNAM'S SONS
New York

A Jeremy P. Tarcher/Putnam Book
Published by G. P. Putnam's Sons
Publishers Since 1838
200 Madison Avenue
New York, NY 10016

The author gratefully acknowledges permission to reprint material from the following sources: *Chieko and Other Poems of Takamura Kōtarō* by Takamura Kōtarō, translated by Hiroaki Seto, © 1980 by The University Press of Hawaii. *The Heart of Awareness: A Translation of the Ashtavakra Gita* by Thomas Byrom, © 1990 by Thomas Byrom, reprinted by arrangement with Shambhala Publications, Inc., 300 Massachusetts Ave., Boston, MA 02115. *Tao Te Ching,* translated by Stephen Mitchell, © 1988 by Stephen Mitchell, reprinted by permission of HarperCollins Publishers, Inc.

Jeremy P. Tarcher, Inc.
5858 Wilshire Blvd., Suite 200
Los Angeles, CA 90036

Published simultaneously in Canada

Library of Congress Cataloging-in-Publication Data

Lasher, Margot
    The art and practice of compassion & empathy / Margot Lasher.—
1st ed.
        p. cm.
    ISBN 0-87477-710-0
    1. Empathy—Problems, exercises, etc. 2. Compassion (Ethics)—Problems, exercises, etc. 3. Meditation. I. Title. II. Title: Art and practice of compassion and empathy.
BF575.E55L37   1992   92-17155 CIP
179'.9—dc20

Cover design by Tanya Maiboroda

Printed in the United States of America

    2   3   4   5   6   7   8   9   10

This book is printed on acid-free paper.
    ∞

For Soren David Pfeffer

CONTENTS

ACKNOWLEDGMENTS

MY TRAINING IN AWARENESS began with dance and Eastern forms of movement. I thank all of my teachers, and the friends with whom I studied.

I have drawn upon the insights of many people who understood compassion and empathy. I have quoted from the writings of some, but others were difficult to quote, and some did not write at all. The perceptual theories of James J. Gibson and Julian Hochberg, and the clinical theories of Heinz Kohut and Jean Baker Miller, have been important to me, as have the writings of Lao Tzu and Carlos Castaneda.

At a more personal level, I have drawn from the insights of Edgar Bourque, Angela Dorenkamp, Lucia Kellar, Soren Pfeffer, and Arlene Vadum. Diane Zeutas-Broer taught me how to use imagery, and Amy Zuckerman helped me with structural decisions. I thank Chris Brouillard, Dana Lasher, Douglas Manfredi, Regula Noetzli, Charles Walker, and my editor, Connie Zweig. I am grateful to everyone at Assumption College for friendship and support. I have learned much from Casey, Manya, the Prince, Hogahn, and Panda. I thank all of you.

PREFACE

Now I live in my heart.
THE ASHTRAVAKRA GITA

If you want to know me,
look inside your heart.
LAO TZU

There is in all things an inexhaustible sweetness and purity, a
silence that is a fountain of action and joy. It rises up in wordless
gentleness and flows out to me from unseen roots of all created
being.

THOMAS MERTON

THERE ARE MOMENTS IN our lives when we sense a special connection to another person. In this connection, we feel perfectly
tuned to the person's feelings. This book is a guide to living
our lives with this sense of connection. In the presence of
compassion and empathy, we are always connected. It is a way
of living in our hearts.

In this book, we will work on creating our own vision of
feelings. With this inner work, we can discover the feelings
that unify us with everything around us. We can feel the connections. Our connections can bring a deep sense of freedom
and inner peace.

In our ordinary lives, most of us feel isolated from other
people, alone and, sometimes, afraid. We feel disconnected
from everything, even from ourselves.

Many aspects of our culture contribute to our sense of isolation. Our culture teaches us to face life alone, to think of dependence as weakness, and to hide our hurts and fears. When
we are isolated, feelings become painful and frightening experiences. Many people have described the pain of feeling separated, and speak of their deep longing for connection.

As human beings, we are all vulnerable. Our longing for connection stems from a deep insight that through connection we transcend our pain. The way of compassion and empathy is a way of experiencing this connection.

> *Empathy is a fundamental mode of human relatedness, the recognition of the self in the other; it is the accepting, confirming and understanding human echo.*
>
> HEINZ KOHUT

> *When your mind is liberated, your heart floods with compassion.*
>
> THICH NHAT HANH

When our friends are peaceful, we feel their calmness inside us. Their peacefulness quiets us. When they are alive and radiant, we sense this aliveness. Their radiance flows into everything, and we feel more alive in their presence.

This is empathy, the echoing within ourselves of another's feelings. This basic response to the inner world of another person represents an incredible human ability. We are tuned to each other's feelings. Our empathic connection is at the center of all of our relationships. It is one of the most intimate ways that we respond to each other.

Compassion is a special case of empathy. When our friends are in pain, we can feel their suffering. And then, in addition to feeling the suffering, we sometimes have an overwhelming feeling of wanting to help them. We want to take away their pain.

This is compassion, the empathic sense of suffering, and the longing to help. Some people feel this connection so strongly that they devote their lives to helping others.

> *Your nature is pure awareness.*
>
> THE ASHTRAVAKRA GITA

> *The touching point, you see, is a point which does not separate one thing from another.*
>
> RAIMUNDO PANIKKAR

All our lives we seek an echoing presence, an empathic being. We find that presence in many different ways, with human beings, with nature, and with spiritual beings. These ways are not independent; they build upon each other in the richness of our inner lives. We find empathy because it is an inseparable part of our existence. The connections are already there, waiting for our awareness.

In this book, empathy is approached as a perceptual ability, like vision and touch. The meaning of our perceptions depends upon our awareness. Clouds are all clouds until we discover that there are distinct shapes, and these shapes are connected to different patterns of wind and rain. The clouds have not changed, and our eyes have not changed; but our vision of the experience has changed dramatically.

The practice of empathy changes our awareness of feelings, our own and the feelings of others. We begin to experience a world in which feelings are as real as cumulus clouds in the natural world. With the practice of empathy, we are creating a vision of feelings.

HOW TO USE THIS BOOK

> *Each of us must make our own true way, and when we do, that way will express the universal way.*
>
> SUZUKI ROSHI

> *I decided to start anew—to strip away what I had been taught, to accept as true my own thinking. This was one of the best times of my life.*
>
> GEORGIA O'KEEFFE

There is an art to living in your heart, and it centers upon the awareness of feelings. This book will help you tune into the world of feelings. The text, the quotations, and the practices are all part of the practice of awareness. You will look at different feelings in different kinds of relationships. In each situation, you will practice being open to whatever is happening within and around you. You will practice being present in the experience, being there empathically.

The techniques for developing compassion and empathy come from ancient spiritual traditions, especially Buddhist and Taoist traditions. But the practice of compassion and empathy does not come from any particular theory or tradition. It belongs to all beings who feel.

Many of the practices in this book involve both memory and imagination. These practices are based upon a form of meditation in which you observe, with quiet awareness, the images in your mind. You can peacefully watch the images that flow through your mind in response to different situations. In the quiet and safety of your inner world, your awareness will deepen.

In many cultures, images from visions and dreams are valid experiences of other realities. There is an acceptance of these other worlds as real. Our own culture finds these realities difficult to accept. But we do accept, to some extent, the reality of an inner world, the world of our minds. We study this mental world in philosophy, psychology and other disciplines. We have developed techniques of awareness.

The imagery techniques in this book belong now to our own as well as other cultures. These techniques are basically universal, because when we seek our inner selves, we find a common reality. We find a reality in which our inner selves meet.

In the practices, I often ask you to imagine, rather than visualize, different situations. In imagining, you can be open to all possible perceptions, especially the perception of feelings. Visualization emphasizes the sense of sight, seeing something in your mind. Visual experience is very strong for most of us, and can sometimes overpower our other senses. But those who are blind have the same awareness of feelings as those who are sighted. Seeing is only one of the ways we are connected to our world.

When you imagine a situation in the practices suggested here, you can let all kinds of images arise: smells and tastes can return you to childhood; the sound of a person's voice can create a delicate vibration within you; a touch on the fine membrane of the skin can generate an emotion. Kinesthetic perception, the sense of your own body, is intricately involved in awareness of feelings. You can tune into all of these perceptions. Actual perceptions and the possibilities of your imagination will merge in the practices. In the richness of this inner world, you will be tuning into feelings.

The meaning of an experience is sometimes not clear until much later. As part of the practices, I will ask you to describe your experiences in a journal. Writing in your journal, and returning later to listen to your own words, can bring you insights. People who spend time in reflection and solitude often keep journals. They use the process of writing to discover things about themselves and their world.

In using this book, you will be exploring a world of feelings. The feelings are sometimes difficult, and experiences involving these feelings may be upsetting to remember. Writing about some experiences can be painful. But it takes energy to hold things in, to keep things from ourselves. Insight gives us greater peacefulness because that energy is freed.

Part of empathic awareness is listening to your own feelings. This book is structured to help you build on unfolding experiences, but you can also, if you choose, read the chapters and do the practices in any order that feels right to you. You can skip any section, or return to any section, at any time. You will find that certain practices bring you a sense of peace or freedom. I hope you will return to these practices often. Let yourself get deeper and deeper into feelings that will help you on your inner journey. You will find your own way.

The journey to compassion and empathy is a journey to a world in which feelings are real connections. In this world, time has only a personal significance. You can bring the past or the future into the present moment. Awareness can come slowly and gradually, as you collect experiences. And it can strike you suddenly, as an insight. The practices in this book are not meant as goals to be achieved. Rather, they are meant to guide you, in your own time and space, to awareness of what is already there, within and around you. Quiet, familiar connections are part of this journey.

The quotations throughout the book represent many of the men and women who committed themselves to an understanding of our inner life and the way of compassion and empathy. I hope that you will feel connected to them through their words.

> *When one reaches this state of harmony between things and one's self, one reaches . . . a state of perfect freedom and peace— which makes everything possible and right. Life becomes perpetual revelation.*
>
> GEORGES BRAQUE

The journey to connection with other people is inseparable from the journey to connection with ourselves. In the way of compassion and empathy presented in this book, a deepening awareness of our own feelings develops in harmony with awareness of the feelings of others. In compassion and empathy we tune in to everything around us: people, the natural world, the spiritual world, and ourselves. When we are in tune, we are connected. The way of compassion and empathy is ultimately a way of union. In the following pages, we will practice this way.

1 COMPASSION AND EMPATHY: BEING OPEN TO FEELINGS

Open yourself to the Tao,
then trust your own response;
and everything will fall into place.

LAO TZU

We need mirroring acceptance, the merger with ideals, the sus-
taining presence of others like us, throughout our lives.

HEINZ KOHUT

It matters immensely. The slightest sound matters. The most
momentary rhythm matters. You can do as you please, yet
everything matters.

WALLACE STEVENS

IMAGINE BEING REALLY OPEN to the world around you. Think
of yourself floating on a raft in the water on a perfect summer
day. You are wonderfully relaxed, open to the motion of the
water which gently rocks you, the touch of the air on your
skin, the feel of the sun.

Imagine now this same sense of openness and freedom between you and another person. You sense whatever the other
person is feeling. The rhythm of this feeling floats through the
air and you allow it to touch you. Your body responds calmly
and acceptingly, so that you actually feel inside you what the
other is feeling.

The journey to empathy is a journey to this way of openness with another person. You are open to feelings.

Sometimes, when the wind catches the tops of tall trees, you
can watch them swaying apart and together in harmony. They
move in response to the same force, expressing its rhythm.
Imagine now that the force comes from inside one of the trees,

I

setting the tree in motion, and then moves outward to the next tree, which responds, echoing the motion.

I believe that our emotional energy acts like these forces. When a friend is feeling happy, we pick up the vibrations and respond in some way. If we are open to the feeling and stay aware, we are being empathic. The energy of the emotion is created, sent out, echoed, and expressed in the harmony of feeling together. It is a natural connection, like trees swaying together.

The image of trees swaying together suggests a special quality of empathy. Empathy, like vision and touch, is a type of perception. In vision, we can see that a friend is happy without feeling that happiness inside us. But in touch, we actually sense the contact with the other person inside the boundary of our body, through our skin. Sometimes we feel a friend's touch as a vibration moving through our spinal column. Empathy is touch at a distance. It is resonance with the other person's feeling. Like the trees, we are actually *moved*.

However, empathic feelings are different in a significant way from feelings which begin inside us as our own. Our minds are highly complex, and we can receive and respond to another's happiness while remaining aware that our feeling of happiness is a response, an echo. We pick up the rhythm of happiness and feel it inside us, while simultaneously recognizing its origin in the other.

We will explore this delicate awareness in the following chapters. Right now, begin the practice of being in tune, starting with the world around you.

BEING IN TUNE WITH THE WORLD AROUND YOU

> *The soul is the world.*   MEISTER ECKHART

> *The hidden harmony is stronger than the visible.*
>   HERACLITUS

I gave myself away to the wind, eastward or westward, like leaves of a tree.

LIEH TZU

Being in tune with other people has much in common with being in tune with the natural world around you. Places have rhythms, and you can pick up the rhythm of a place and feel connected to it. The rhythm of ocean waves can calm or excite you; so can the expanse of sky at the top of a mountain or the sense of the earth in the center of a meadow. When you pick up the rhythm of a place, your body tunes into that place, and your own natural rhythms—such as breathing and heartbeat—fall into harmony with that rhythm.

In many of the practices in this book, I will ask you to close your eyes and imagine yourself in a certain setting. You will enter the world of memory and imagination, the world of your mind. In the first practice, I want you to feel, in your mind, your connection to the natural world. You will be able to sense the rhythms of the surrounding world, which is in motion, and the connection between these rhythms and the rhythms inside you. These rhythms establish feelings at the most basic level: calmness or agitation, safety or fear.

Practice 1

FEELING THE RHYTHM OF A PLACE

Imagine yourself in a natural setting, someplace where you feel comfortable and safe. This place does not have to be real. It can be a place in your mind, perhaps an ideal place for you. It could be at the ocean, on a mountaintop, in a small meadow, any place where you feel safe and free.

Close your eyes and imagine yourself in that setting. Take a few minutes to transport yourself to that place. Feel the air on your skin, the ground under your feet. If there is motion in the water or the sky, let it inside you. If there is a breeze, let it touch you. If there is sun, let it warm you.

Something about this place brings you peace and lets you be free. Your body responds to the rhythm. You are picking up a rhythm that creates a feeling of peacefulness inside you. It might be the rhythm of a breeze or the rhythm of flowing water. You are responding to the feeling of the place by allowing that feeling to enter and connect inside you. You have become aware of the connection between the setting and yourself. You are feeling the rhythm of that place.

Head a page of your journal "Feeling the Rhythm of a Place." Write down all of the sensations of touch, warmth, floating or rocking, whatever you experienced in your ideal place. Now list on the left-hand side of the page all the feelings that came to you in that place. If you felt peaceful, alive, comfortable, write down those feelings. If you felt fear or confusion, write those feelings down. Become aware of all of your feelings. All of your feelings in that place are part of your connection to it. What things about the place made you feel safe? What made you feel free? What made you feel afraid? Next to each feeling, write down anything about the place that created that feeling.

UNUSUAL EXPERIENCES OF COMPASSION AND EMPATHY

Music, states of happiness, mythology, faces scored by time, certain places, all want to tell us something, or told us something we should not have missed, or are about to tell us something.
JORGE LUIS BORGES

And while I stood there I saw more than I can tell and I understood more than I saw; for I was seeing in a sacred manner. . . .
BLACK ELK

Experiences of compassion and empathy can be rare encounters that shake us into awareness, and they also can be quiet moments in our ordinary life that bring gradual awareness. We will look first at the unusual experience.

We have all had intense, sudden connections with another person, and we remember them vividly because they are so emotionally powerful. An unusual experience of empathy or compassion often becomes a touchstone in our lives. It stands apart from our ordinary life, and can change our understanding of ourselves at the deepest level. In the next few practices, you can recall these unusual experiences in your life.

An Unusual Experience of Empathy

Unusual experiences of empathy often come to us in childhood, when we are more open to the feelings around us. Think for a few moments about your early memories. These memories can be very strong. You might have an image from childhood in which you suddenly felt a connection with your father or mother that changed your perception of them. You might have sensed at some moment that your strong, stoic father was feeling fear, and that moment may live in your mind as a bond between you. There may have been a moment when your mother, who was usually reserved and sad, suddenly experienced a sense of freedom, and you were with her and felt that change. These are moments of unusual empathic awareness.

Practice 2

AN UNUSUAL EXPERIENCE OF EMPATHY

Recall any experience of unusual emotional connection that comes to you. Let whatever emotions you felt at the time return to you. Relive the experience.

Head a page of your journal "An Unusual Experience of Empathy." Describe your experience in the journal. Write down any details you see in your mind about yourself, the other person, and the connection between you. Write down all of your feelings during the experience. These details can be important in developing your awareness of empathy in your life.

An Unusual Experience of Compassion

Because compassion is a special case of empathy, your experiences of these connections are going to overlap a great deal, and it is not important that you keep them separate. What is important right now are your memories of significant moments of emotional connection. These memories are your touchstones.

In a strong experience of compassion, another person is suffering and you feel the suffering inside you. You feel so connected that you want to help the other person as if he were yourself. These are the two emotions in compassion: the empathic feeling of suffering, and the desire to help. A story in Buddhist teachings captures the essence of the unusual experience of compassion.

One day a king saw a bull being led to slaughter. As he watched the bull, he suddenly felt a powerful connection to this great creature, so strong and alive and now so frightened. He called out, "Let it go!" saving the bull's life. Later, the king asked a wise man to tell him the secret of being a true king. The wise man reminded him of his experience with the bull. If you could have those feelings for all of the people, the wise man told him, you would not let anyone die of starvation or be killed in a war, and you would be a true king.

Practice 3

An Unusual Experience of Compassion

Recall an event in your life when you felt a strong, unifying sense of compassion. It might be connected to a person or an animal. It might be from childhood. Remember the feeling of compassion as you experienced it. Relive the experience.

Head a page of your journal "An Unusual Experience of Compassion." Write down your experience of the event. Include any details that come to you. Did you feel a desire to help? Were you able to help? Let all of your feelings about the event come out. If you wanted to act but were stopped by someone, you may feel anger or pain. That is natural. Write about the situation now, remembering that you are not a king who can command others at will. But there are situations in which you can help, sometimes by just being there and staying open to the other person's pain.

ORDINARY MOMENTS OF EMPATHY AND COMPASSION

> *For the person who is aware, breakthrough does not happen once a year, once a month, once a day, but many times every day.*
> MEISTER ECKHART

> *Everything we come across is to the point.*   JOHN CAGE

You can experience compassion and empathy as integral parts of your ordinary life. Reliving the unusual experiences will strengthen your awareness of the subtle moments of more everyday connections. You already have these connections to everything around you; it is just a matter of becoming more aware of the feelings that are the source of the connection. This awareness of daily connections will bring a sense of clarity and serenity that will enable you, if and when you feel ready, to make wider connections. There is no pressure here, no need to push. If you start with familiar, quiet connections, the rest will flow naturally.

Practice 4

AN EMPATHIC CONNECTION IN MY DAILY LIFE

For this practice, think of someone with whom you are comfortable. It might be a child, a close friend, a sister, or brother. It is someone you see in a natural, ordinary way as part of your normal life so that you are at ease and can be yourself with them.

Close your eyes, relax, and imagine yourself with them. You are in the same room together, not necessarily doing the same thing, not necessarily talking. Sense the connection between you. It is a comfortable connection. Try to sense what makes you feel comfortable. Is the other person responsive to your feelings? Are you especially open to the other person's feelings? Is empathy—your own and the other's—part of the connection between you? Try to feel, not so much in words but in the quality of sensations, what this connection is like for you.

Head a page of your journal "An Empathic Connection in My Daily Life." Write down the name of the person and the sensations you have when you are with them. The translation from feelings to words is difficult and usually inadequate, so don't get upset if you cannot translate the essence of the connection. The important thing is that you have identified someone in your daily life with whom you have an empathic connection.

EMPTYING THE SELF

> *Let yourself dissolve.*
> THE ASHTRAVAKRA GITA

> *Be you compassionate as your Father in heaven is compassionate.*
>
> JESUS

> *The old Lacandon medicine man Chan Kin Viego offered respect not only to the plants and creatures of the rainforest but also to those who have destroyed them as well. This capacity to practice reconciliation by seeing through the eyes of another, whether creature, plant, environmental feature, or man is frequently encountered in the tribal world.*
>
> JOAN HALIFAX

We have been practicing opening ourselves to the world around us. In Buddhist meditation, this practice is often called the *emptying of the self.* Emptying the self is at the center of Buddhist meditation, and many of the practices in this book are based on this tradition.

When we open ourselves to the world around us, our way of experiencing the self changes. When we tune into the rhythms of the natural world, we are dissolving the boundaries of the self. When we empathically echo another person's feeling, we are becoming free of the sense of being an isolated self. In the practice of empathy, we are emptying the self to receive the world.

The emptying of the self is a central aspect of spiritual traditions. If we are filled up with ourselves, there is no room to receive a spiritual presence. It is also essential for compassion. Filled with ourselves, we cannot let in the suffering of others. Focused upon our own pain, we do not have the energy to give to another. When we are able to empty ourselves, we open ourselves to those around us, including those who are in pain.

The emptying of the self can be practiced in many ways. In Native American and Shinto traditions, the self is spiritually inseparable from the natural world. In these traditions, spiritual places are natural places—mountains, bodies of water, the sky. In Japan, a Shinto shrine is a lean-to, open to the elements. The shrine is often built at the top of the highest hill, overlooking the village and close to the sky. People climb the hill alone and communicate in solitude. They feel at one with the natural world.

In medieval Christianity, emptying the self was understood in a different context. In Christopher Marlowe's *Doctor Faustus,* a tragedy based upon a medieval folk legend, Faustus commits sin after sin against God. But all of these sins are human, and would be nothing in the presence of God's compassion. Faustus's tragedy is that he is so filled with thoughts of himself, so focused on his past, that he cannot let God forgive him. His sin is despair. He closes himself off from his compassionate God. He cannot empty himself to let God in.

A MEDITATIVE APPROACH TO
EMPTYING THE SELF

> *Be mindful that you are in the universe and the universe is in you: if the universe is, you are: if you are, the universe is.*
> THICH NHAT HANH

> *You must be nothing but an ear that hears what the universe of the word is constantly saying within you.*
> DOV BAER OF MEZRITCH

> *Just space is left—lovely, lovely space going on forever. That space stays long if you can do without you. Not you and space, you see; just space, no you.*
> AH CHENG (QUOTED BY JOHN BLOFELD)

Imagine that you are upset; it doesn't matter why. You go to a quiet place, sit still, and begin to relax. Just as you are beginning to breathe peacefully, a sound starts coming from outside. A neighbor is hammering. You are disturbed by the sound and begin to feel tense and upset all over again.

You could focus intensely on something else, and eventually your awareness of the hammering would disappear. Your mind has the ability to block out perceptions. There are many ordinary examples of this blocking, as when you stop hearing the hissing of a radiator after you have been in a room for a while.

There is another way of responding, however, that develops a sense of openness that is essential to compassion and empathy. In this way, you practice staying open to whatever happens, receiving and observing. In the case of the hammering, you let it enter. You let the sound flow through you. The key to this method is that you do not resist.

The art of Tai Chi is the perfect embodiment of non-resistance. In Tai Chi, when someone attacks you, you yield. By bending and softening your body, you neutralize or actually avoid the blow. Your opponent, who expects to be met by the bulk of your body and its force, is thrown off balance. You remain safe and balanced by yielding.

In sitting quietly, you can yield to any perceptions, including thoughts and feelings. You can imagine yourself as a fluid, open space. The sound of the hammering flows through you. So do the upsetting thoughts and feelings. You yield to them, and they flow by. You remain balanced and peaceful.

In the following practice, you can begin to experience the emptying of the self in this way.

Practice 5

EMPTYING THE SELF

Sit quietly in a place where you feel comfortable and safe. Breathe deeply, and let your body relax. Imagine the tension in your body leaving you with each outgoing breath. Now breathe quietly. Let yourself feel the peaceful rhythm of your breath entering and leaving.

Listen to any sounds coming from outside you. Pick up some sound—the wind, a radiator, traffic—and listen to that sound. Imagine it entering and settling in your mind. Sense what it feels like to let it settle in your mind.

Now imagine that it begins to move. It is a stream that is flowing from outside, through the space of your mind, and out again. Sense the difference between the sound settling inside you and the sound as a stream passing through you. Play with the sound, sometimes letting it settle and sometimes letting it just flow through.

Try the same image with your own thoughts. Let a thought rise in your mind and float out again.

Imagine yourself as a quiet, empty space, letting sounds and thoughts flow through you.

THE QUALITY OF ATTENTION

When awareness is completely balanced, communicating with the outside world is instantaneous and automatic. It happens with the touch of thought.

DEEPAK CHOPRA

Every time we pay attention we become emptier, and the more empty we are, the more healing space we can offer.
DONALD MCNEILL, DOUGLAS MORRISON,
AND HENRI NOUWEN

Attention is a process of selection. We select, from the incredible variety of the world around us, one or two aspects to attend to. We choose the sound of a friend's voice over the other voices in the room. We choose our inner voice, sometimes, listening to our own thoughts rather than to external voices.

Selective attention is a natural part of perception. The difficulty occurs when we begin to block out aspects of our world because of habit. We select too early, out of habit. When we act or think or feel habitually, we are closed to the unknown. We are closed to everything outside of our ordinary world.

In one of his lectures to analysts in training, Freud describes the kind of attention he gives to his patients. He says that he listens with "evenly hovering attention." He meant that he tries not to select from the different kinds of communication coming from the patient. His mind hovers evenly, receiving each sound and silence, what is said, the way it is said, and when it is said.

To listen in this way, we have to be open. We have to be able to suspend judgment. We have to be receptive to all possibilities, not just those we have anticipated based upon preconceptions. This is a delicate, intricate skill. It is the psychological equivalent of emptying the self.

Karen Horney, a colleague of Freud's who studied Eastern meditation, described this quality of attention as "whole-heartedness of attention." We are there with all of ourselves and, at the same time, we forget ourselves. We are so absorbed in the other person that we lose the sense of our self. This, also, is part of the emptying of the self.

A friend of mine noticed that the word Horney chose, *whole-heartedness,* means being there with all of your heart. You are there in the connection with the other person *with all your feelings.* This is the quality of attention that we want to practice in empathy. We want to be tuned to feelings. This includes our own feelings as well as the other person's, because our own feelings are part of the energy flowing between us. We want to be there, with the other person, completely absorbed in that connection between us. When we are really absorbed, we no longer sense two separated selves.

Practice 6

WHOLEHEARTEDNESS OF ATTENTION

The purpose of this practice is to experience wholehearted-ness of attention in a familiar way. Think of the things you do that you thoroughly enjoy. Some people love to garden, for example. They get out in the earth and the sun and work for hours, fully absorbed in the job. Some people play an instrument. When they are playing, they are one with the instrument and the sound.

I spoke once to an American who defected to China dur-ing the Korean War and lived there for thirteen years. He said that the only time when he didn't think of himself as a foreigner was when he was playing basketball. During a game, he did not feel different from the other players. They were all there in the movement, working as one.

Think of something that gives you this sense of com-plete absorption. The next time you do this activity, do it as always. If you start thinking about the quality of your at-tention while you are doing it, your attention will be divided.

Take your journal with you, and immediately after-wards, if you can, begin to write. Head a page of your journal "Wholeheartedness of Attention," and describe the sense of being completely absorbed. Did you have a sense of yourself as separate from the activity? Did you forget yourself? Were you thinking about the time, what you did yesterday or needed to do tomorrow? Or were you fully present in the moment? Did you feel that you and the activity were one?

UNIFYING STRUCTURES IN YOUR LIFE

All the arts we practice are apprenticeship. The big art is our life.
                                                    M. C. RICHARDS

*I don't write about things. I write from inside of something, and
I sing and play the same way. It's never about that something,
hoping to touch it. It's rather from the inside of it reaching out.*
                                                    BOB DYLAN

With the practices in this first chapter you have begun to
discover what being connected means to you, and what things
about a person or a place enable you to feel comfortable and
safe in being connected. You also may have remembered an
unusual, especially powerful experience of empathy or compassion. Recall the story of the king who identified so strongly
with the frightened bull. He was open to the animal's feelings,
open to receiving inside himself the terror and helplessness
and desire to live, and he cried out with all the strength of these
feelings, saving the animal's life. This was an unusual, touchstone experience of compassion in his life.

Yet the meaning of the experience in his life as a whole was
not clear to him until much later. This is often the case with
significant experiences. We sometimes need time, and the
practice of awareness, to understand.

Your journal is a way of returning to experiences in reflection. In reading through your journal at a later time, you can
find new meaning in your descriptions, connecting images and
memories into more coherent, illuminating structures. These
unifying structures will enable you to be more open to present
feelings. They will help you to integrate all parts of yourself.

Carlos Castaneda makes a distinction between ordinary and
nonordinary reality. An inner journey is part of nonordinary
reality. In nonordinary reality, we begin to discover unusual
connections. These connections may be with places or with
people, or with parts of ourselves.

Practice 7

A UNIFYING STRUCTURE IN MY LIFE

Read the entries you made in your journal from the six practices in this chapter. Find anything that seems to be a link between two or more of the entries. This link could be a recurring feeling, a sensation, a physical presence— anything at all. Let whatever it is strike you intuitively and naturally; let it come as an insight. Don't try to analyze your entries in any scientific or critical way. Just stay with the first unifying structure that comes to you.

Head a page in your journal "A Unifying Structure in My Life." Write down the connection you saw between the journal entries. It is enough to just write down the structure. But if you feel like it, you can also say what this unifying structure means to you now, at this moment.

In the next chapter we will look at the fears we may have about being emotionally connected to others. We are afraid of losing our selves. In the context of empathy and compassion, we will be able to see this fear in a new way.

2 FEARS ABOUT COMPASSION AND EMPATHY

*Absorption is all that we have enumerated: a concentrated atten-
tion, a self-forgetfulness or self-emptying, a giving oneself completely to the matter or situation at hand, a merging with it.*

CLAUDIO NARANJO

I perhaps owe having become a painter to flowers.

CLAUDE MONET

*How many of these places in space have already been within me.
Many a wind is like a son to me.*

RAINER MARIA RILKE

*A Poet . . . has no Identity—he is continually . . . filling
some other Body—the Sun, the Moon, the Sea and Men and
Women.*

JOHN KEATS

SOME PEOPLE, IN THINKING about compassion and empathy,
feel afraid of losing themselves in a connection with another
person. They fear being overwhelmed by the other person's
emotions.

There are two different experiences of the loss of self. One
is the experience of being so perfectly connected to another
that we transcend the sense of the isolated self. This experience brings feelings of complete safety and inner peace. Para-
doxically, this loss of self brings us the sense of finally finding
our real self.

In this chapter we are going to talk about the opposite experience; the terrible, frightening loss of the sense of who we

are. This fear of losing identity is real and powerful. It is based on the truth that we are physically and psychologically vulnerable creatures. We suffer, and eventually we face our own death.

Just as we understand the vulnerability of our children and act to protect them, we also act to protect ourselves. One of the ways we protect ourselves is self-empathy—knowing ourselves and listening to our feelings. A second way we protect ourselves is self-compassion—knowing our own suffering and acting to take ourselves out of danger.

The way of compassion and empathy that I am presenting is only possible through the practice of self-understanding and the development of inner strength. The difference between this way and many of our cultural beliefs is that self-understanding and inner strength come through connection. They come through interaction with one's own self, with other people, with animals and the natural world, and with spiritual presence. Our empathic and compassionate connections lead to the strengthening and deepening of the sense of self.

OUR FEAR THAT EMPATHY LEADS TO THE LOSS OF OUR SELF

> . . . *Above all, do not*
> *plant me in your heart. I should grow too fast.*
> RAINER MARIA RILKE

> *Hold on to the center.*
> LAO TZU

Imagine that you are with someone who is constantly depressed. You are understandably afraid that if you remain empathically open, this depression will seep into you and permeate your being. You will lose your center and become depressed.

You can have the same fear if you are the one who is sad or

upset and the other person is closed to your feelings and determined to be happy at all costs. If you open yourself to this other person's feelings, you lose the ability to feel and explore your own sadness. Again, you are afraid of losing your own center by giving in to the other.

In both of these examples, the problem is that the other person is unable to be empathic. All of their attention is focused on the struggle occurring within themselves.

If you know, or hope, that this is a temporary situation, usually you will not be afraid. You know that the person is going through a difficult time, and you wait. But if the person is *never* able to be empathic, you need to face that. If you are afraid of being swallowed up by the person's emotions, if some part of your self is warning you of danger, you need to listen and to act.

One of the most important things to remember about empathy is that it is a form of perception. And perception is listening and seeing, being aware and understanding the world.

To experience empathy as a way of understanding, imagine that it is a late summer afternoon, and you are standing on a beach watching the gentle motion of the waves. You perceive the waves, their visual pattern and the pattern of their sound, and you let this rhythm inside you. Your body tunes into the gentle rhythm and it calms you.

Now imagine that a storm is approaching from the ocean. The light becomes eerie; the wind picks up. The air and water become agitated. You watch these changes as you stand on the beach. You allow the new rhythm inside you and you feel a sense of excitement from the approaching storm. Your body tunes into the rhythm of the storm.

The storm is now close upon you. The wind begins to gust and the waves heighten. Your excitement changes to fear. Your fear is real. You see that the storm is almost upon you, and you know that the beach is a dangerous place to be during a storm. Your fear and your knowledge of the ocean both tell you to protect yourself. You take shelter.

You want to be open to the world around you. You want to be able to feel the calm of a placid ocean, and the excitement of the wind and waves. You want to be free to tune into the rhythms of nature.

But you also want to protect yourself from potential danger. And here empathy for yourself is crucial. Because when you begin to feel fear, you must listen to your feelings. You must be open to all your feelings and be ready to protect yourself.

Feeling and thinking occur together as a natural, automatic connection in our minds. You are feeling the rhythm of the ocean and thinking about it at the same time. When everything is peaceful, your mind can be peaceful. When the storm is close, you perceive the rough waves and gusting wind; you feel fear, and you think: "This is a dangerous situation." You do not stop thinking because you are feeling. You do not stop thinking because you are empathically open.

In the same way, imagine that you are caring for a young child and you sense empathically that something is wrong. You do not know what it is; you just have a feeling that the child is suffering. You are empathically open, sensing some danger. But you do not lose your center in the feelings. You are unified with the child in your feelings; you sense the suffering inside you, and you want to remove it. But you do not *become* the child, who is in pain but too young to understand. You remain aware of everything, thinking about the situation, trying to figure out what is wrong. Then, as an adult, you act in some way to help the child.

Practice 8

PROTECTING MYSELF FROM THE STORM

Close your eyes, relax, and imagine yourself in the scene at the ocean described above. You are standing on the beach in late summer, late afternoon. If you are more familiar with inland storms, change the scene to a prairie or mountains and imagine yourself there.

Imagine yourself responding to the three conditions of the landscape: the peaceful late afternoon, the changes in light and the other signs of the approaching storm, then the storm almost upon you. Respond within yourself to the different rhythms of the scene. Think about your feelings in each condition. When you feel real danger, imagine doing whatever you need to do to protect yourself.

Head a page of your journal "Protecting Myself from the Storm." Describe each of your feelings in relation to the landscape and the storm. Do you have a different sense of self when you are peaceful and when you are frightened? Can you feel the difference between being open and then closing yourself off for self-protection? Describe how you protected yourself when you felt the danger. This self-protection is a natural survival response, and the purpose of this practice is simply to enable you to become more aware of your own resources.

Practice 9

PROTECTING MYSELF FROM ANOTHER PERSON'S EMOTIONS

Now, I would like you to repeat Practice 8 in a situation with another person. You can use a real memory or simply imagine a scene as you imagined the storm. For most of us, real memories and imagined scenes mix together in this kind of practice.

Imagine three conditions in your scene with the other person. At first, things are calm and relaxed between you. You are empathically open. Then something excites or disturbs the situation. You are still empathically open, but you are thinking and aware of the nature of the disturbance. Finally, you sense the presence of danger. Try to imagine an emotional rather than a physical danger. You feel fear. Remain empathically open to your own feeling of fear. Imagine protecting your self from the emotional danger. Do whatever you need to protect your self from losing your center, from losing your self.

Head a page of your journal "Protecting Myself from Another Person's Emotions." Describe the scene between you and the other person. Describe your sense of your self in each condition: calm, excited or disturbed, and sensing danger. Were you able to remain open to your own sense of danger? This is empathy for yourself. How did you protect yourself?

It is natural and wise to protect yourself. The key is remaining aware of the self and the other, and staying open to your sense of fear and the approach of danger. The key is empathy for your self.

OUR FEAR THAT COMPASSION WILL LEAD TO CONSTANT SUFFERING

If you are mindful of death, it will not come as a surprise—you will not be anxious. You will feel that death is merely like changing clothes. Consequently, at that point you will be able to maintain your calmness of mind.

THE DALAI LAMA

I believe in person to person; every person is Christ for me, and since there is only one Jesus, that person is the one person in the world at that moment.

MOTHER TERESA

A caricature of the compassionate person is someone walking through life relentlessly looking for pain. This person saves the lives of two hundred bugs, five animals and at least one human per day. In this stereotype there is no play or laughter.

There are very special people who work constantly with extraordinary amounts of suffering and pain. But these unusual people do not feel constant suffering. They have evolved a way of being in the world that enables them to transcend the personal feeling of suffering. They are connected to a spiritual presence that brings them peace and even playfulness.

The practices in this book will not help anyone to reach

sainthood. The practices suggest ways that compassion can grow through connections that are already part of your life: children, friends, parents, an intimate companion.

It does happen, however, that as you practice compassion, it becomes easier, more natural, more part of your way of seeing the world. Morgan Grey said that when you begin to see many possibilities as spiritual, your world becomes spiritual. It is the same with compassion.

A doctor once told me that before he recommends a medical procedure, he asks himself what he would do if the person were his own mother or father. He did not mean that he suffers with each patient the way he would suffer if his mother or father were seriously ill. He meant that he experiences each situation from within as well as from without before acting. Compassion was already part of his way of being in his personal world. He was able to extend that way of understanding to his patients.

OUR FEAR OF BEING INTRUSIVE AND INTERFERING

> *Compassion simply stated is leaving other people alone. You don't lay trips.*
>
> RAM DASS

> *Doing something about a problem which you do not understand is like trying to clear away darkness by thrusting it aside with your hands. When light is brought, the darkness vanishes at once.*
>
> ALAN WATTS

> *Practice not-doing,*
> *and everything will fall into place.*
> LAO TZU

The third fear which I want to talk about is the fear that empathy and compassion intrude on privacy—our own and another person's. It is the fear that empathy will fail to respect boundaries and compassion will interfere in another's life. This fear comes from confusion about the nature of empathy.

Empathy is the perception and echoing of feelings. Imagine that you walk into a room and a close friend is there. You sense empathically that something is wrong. You ask her what is wrong and she says "nothing."

At this point you could insist that something is wrong. This would be insisting on the accuracy of your perception. *It would not be empathy.* Empathy is tuning into the other person's feelings. It is perceiving her situation from the inside, and staying open in order to understand. It is sensing that something is wrong, and also sensing that she does not want to talk at that moment. This is all part of seeing the situation from her framework.

Empathy is perceptual, like vision and touch. When we look at someone, we are normally not intrusive. The other person does not feel invaded or controlled by our perception. But in some situations, when the person does not want to be seen, out looking *is* intrusive. With any form of perception, we have to know how to respect boundaries. If we are really being empathic, we will have this respect because we will sense the other person's discomfort. We will feel empathically their need to be left alone.

When someone tells me that a friend is being empathically intrusive, I am disturbed. In my understanding, this is not possible. If someone is empathically attuned, they will not be intrusive.

It is the same with compassion. Compassion begins with empathic perception: the sensing of suffering. When someone is suffering, there is a desire to help them. But there are many situations in which wisdom, or some other grace, tells us to leave them alone. My friend's grandmother, who was in her nineties, was in the hospital and refusing food. My friend was trying to force her to eat when the doctor suggested that perhaps this was her way of easing into dying. Elisabeth Kubler-Ross has told us that sometimes a dying person will hold on, with enormous suffering, because a loved one cannot let them go. Compassion can be letting go, letting someone be, acting by not acting. Each situation is different and the complexities of any one situation can be enormous. Compassion, when it is really sensing the suffering from within, is not interfering.

Practice 10

LETTING-BE THROUGH EMPATHY

In this practice, recall a situation in which you felt that someone did not want to be looked at. The person may have been ill and did not want you to see them in that condition. They may have been so upset that any contact, visual or otherwise, was too much for them at that moment. Recall the situation and your feeling that they did not want to be seen. Relive the experience, including your own feelings.

Head a page of your journal "Letting-be through Empathy." Describe the situation and your feeling that they did not want to be seen. Were you able to give them their privacy? Was it difficult for you to not look? How did you feel about letting them alone?

Practice 11

LETTING-BE THROUGH COMPASSION

In this practice I would like you to recall a situation in which you sensed that someone was struggling and you wanted to help, but you held yourself back. You sensed that doing something would be more upsetting to the other person than letting them alone.

Relive the experience, focusing especially on the moment when you held yourself back. What were you feeling at that moment?

Head a page of your journal "Letting-be through Compassion." Were you aware of two things: sensing the other person's suffering, and sensing that they did not want to be

helped? Did you feel a conflict inside yourself between help-
ing and not helping? Or did you have a clear insight that
not helping was best? What kind of understanding of the
person and the situation enabled you not to interfere?

I hope that in the last two practices you have seen that letting someone be is part of empathy and compassion. It is part of seeing the situation from the other person's perspective. It is difficult to remember this because, in our culture, empathy is often seen as feeling sorry for someone, and compassion is seen as taking pity on them. We are surrounded by these ideas, ones that are based upon a vision of the world in which we are all separate, competitive beings. And those who suffer are thought to be lower than those who do not.

There is another vision of the world in which we are connected, and wisdom and strength come through a deepening awareness of our connectedness. In this vision empathy is a perceptual ability that enables an understanding of a situation from inside the other person. Compassion is the special case in which the other person is suffering and our feeling of connection leads us to want to help. But if we remain open to the other person's feelings, sensing how they are experiencing the situation, compassion can be letting them alone, letting them work things out for themselves, acting by not acting. Everything depends upon the situation and the connection between you.

In the next chapter we will look further at ideas that block our feelings of compassion and empathy. We are working on seeing the world and our connections to others in a new way. We are working on a vision of feelings.

3 IDEAS THAT BLOCK COMPASSION AND EMPATHY

How do I know this is true?
I look inside myself and see.
LAO TZU

Now all my teachers are dead except silence.

W. S. MERWIN

MOST OF US WHO grew up in Western culture have accepted a certain way of looking at the world. As children, though, we usually saw our world very differently. Our minds were free to see and accept many different realities. As we grew older, we often dismissed these insights as fantasy and make-believe. All of us, however, still carry within us our inherent freedom of mind. But most of us have chosen, in our actions at least, to fit in with the framework of our culture.

Our ability to see other realities is always with us. Sometimes it lies dormant for a time and will suddenly be awakened by some small event—meeting a person or having a daydream. The experience transports us to a way of understanding which is different but familiar. We have a sense of returning to a lost part of ourselves.

This chapter discusses some ideas that are dominant in our culture, ones that most of us at some level have been pressured to accept. We accept them because we have to live with them: they are pervasive in our society. These ideas close us off to compassion and empathy. That is why we have to question them now.

In the practices, think about how each idea has affected your life. You might think of a specific event, perhaps a time when your mother or father hurt you because of their acceptance of this idea. You might think of a time when you acted toward another person in a certain way because you thought it was the only acceptable way, even when part of you wanted to act differently. As you read about each way of thinking, you will probably remember some influence on your own life.

Then write about your experiences in your journal. Describe how each way of thinking affected you. It may have affected your thoughts, feelings, actions, or all of these, intertwined together. Write down whatever memories and feelings come to you as you read about these ideas. Your feelings are especially important because all of these practices, no matter what their content, are ways of becoming more open to feelings.

THE IDEA OF THE ISOLATED SELF

> *Our mistake has been to suppose that the individual is honored and his uniqueness enhanced by emphasizing his separation from the surrounding world, or his eternal difference in essence from his Creator.*
>
> ALAN WATTS

> *By investigating and integrating the different levels at which we create duality—the shadow and persona, the identification with the ego-mind and the body, the dichotomy of self and other—we come to the experience of freedom.*
>
> JOSEPH GOLDSTEIN

In modern Western culture there is a strong tendency to see the self as an isolated entity. This view stems from a philosophical doubt about the reality of anything outside of the subjective self. The ancient Greeks, in exploring perception, discovered what they called the *illusions* of the senses. If the world is composed of tiny, invisible particles of energy in motion, then the world of the senses, the world of solid objects and colors and sounds, is an elaborate illusion. We are trapped in our own bodies, never knowing reality.

But in almost all cultures, this initial doubt developed into an understanding that there were many different possible realities: the world of sense perception, the world of scientific explanation, the world of thought. And in all cultures, there is a spiritual possibility, enabling us to experience the wholeness of reality, and the unity of the self with the whole.

In our culture, however, the world of science alone is accepted as the world of reality. If the Western scientific method cannot find evidence for the existence of something, it is declared unreal. In this framework, empathic connections are not real, and the individual self is essentially isolated from any true emotional or spiritual connection with others.

This view of science as the only reality is a phase of our intellectual history that seems to be slowly grinding to a halt. But all of us have been affected by it in some way. It has blocked our awareness of compassion and empathy.

Practice 12

How the Idea of the Isolated Self Has Affected My Life

Think about how the image of the isolated self has affected your life. Have you had empathic feelings which you or another person have dismissed as illusions? Have you had intuitions, or extra-sensory perceptions, that you have rejected as unscientific and therefore unreal? Have you felt isolated from others because they would not allow you to talk about these experiences?

Head a page of your journal "How the Idea of the Isolated Self Has Affected My Life." Describe how you have been affected by this way of thinking.

THE IDEA OF AUTONOMY

No man is an island.   JOHN DONNE

*If we can allow ourselves to feel vulnerable and insecure when
that is what is arising, if we can be totally ourselves without any
pretense, we will find a great inner strength.*

JOSEPH GOLDSTEIN

*For man has closed himself up, till he sees all things thro' narrow
chinks of his cavern.*

WILLIAM BLAKE

In the context of our culture, with the self essentially isolated from others, it was necessary to develop a psychology in
which the person could survive and find some sense of freedom and completion within the framework of isolation. The
theory that developed was the theory of autonomy.

According to this theory, the infant begins in almost total dependence upon another and childhood is a gradual process of
developing a self and separating that self from the other person. The path to full adulthood is the path to autonomy: not
needing anyone else, conquering fear and loneliness, standing
strong, separate, and complete within oneself.

We all have times of fear and suffering. The path of autonomy trains us to hide these feelings, to conquer this weakness
by denying the feelings, both in ourselves and in the other person who might need us. Autonomy tells us to say to our children things like "Big boys don't cry," and "Grown-up girls
aren't afraid of the dark." The fear, of course, doesn't disappear; it goes inward, and the child learns to hide it. We hide our
vulnerability, and in this hiding, we lose the heart of ourselves.
We pretend, even to ourselves, that we don't need connections
to others.

The idea of autonomy blocks the natural development of
compassion and empathy. On the path of compassion, we
would pick up the little boy and hold him until the pain went

away. We would stay with the little girl in the dark so that she knew that we understood her fear. We would show our children that vulnerability is an inseparable part of human existence, and they are not alone.

When the goal of human life is autonomy, the natural, quiet flow of empathic perception and unifying compassion is effectively crushed. The ideal adult is seen as independent of others. In this context, awareness of what is happening inside another person is unimportant. The intimate connection created by an echoing response is seen only as weakness. So the idea of autonomy turns compassion and empathy into signs of immaturity, the lack of a fully developed sense of self.

Of course there are many, many people who do not accept this way of thinking. There is, for example, a group of psychologists, including Jean Baker Miller, Judith Jordan, Andrea Kaplan, Irene Stiver and Janet Surrey, who are currently working on a self-in-relation theory. In this theory the self develops in connection with others, and empathy is one of the most significant aspects of this connection. In many spiritual traditions, openness to feelings, in oneself and in others, is an essential step on the path to real understanding. In both psychological and spiritual traditions, openness to feelings is part of the way to inner strength and freedom.

Practice 13

How the Idea of Autonomy Has Affected My Life

Think about how the idea of autonomy has affected your own development. Did your father or mother allow you to express fear and vulnerability? Did they teach you to hide these feelings? As an adult, does part of you feel that being connected to another person is a weakness, and you ought to be able to stand alone?

Head a page of your journal "How the Idea of Autonomy Has Affected My Life." Write down whatever you have been thinking and feeling about the idea of autonomy.

THE IDEA OF OPPOSING POLES: EMPATHIC AND NONEMPATHIC

Instead of creating solid things, solid relations, a solid, unchanging world to try to hold on to, we can let go and open to the actual truth of each changing moment.

JACK KORNFIELD

Everything already exists in a state of tranquility. However, this state of tranquility is masked from us by our assumption that there is a separation, that there is a problem.

SUZUKI ROSHI

In our culture human qualities are often characterized by opposing poles. In this way of thinking, you are either empathic or not empathic, and the many subtle ways of being partially empathic are ignored. At the beginning of a workshop on empathy, a man told me that he was not empathic, and he didn't even know what the word meant. To try to explain it, I began talking about animals: how they pick up our energy and echo it—when I get excited, my dog gets excited too. I could see the man's eye widen, and his whole body became alive. His dog had been sick and had died recently. He had felt inside him a sense of life and happiness in the brief moments when she was free from pain, and he had suffered when she was suffering. He had been empathic in this special situation with his dog.

We are not empathic or nonempathic in some extreme, unchanging way. We are sometimes empathic, in some situations, with some people and some animals. We can experience all shades of empathic openness even with the same person. We can and do grow in our empathic ability. As the man remembered his connection to the dog and felt its reality, he saw the possibilities of empathy in other aspects of his life.

Practice 14

HOW THINKING OF MYSELF AS EITHER EMPATHIC OR NONEMPATHIC HAS AFFECTED MY LIFE

Have you thought of yourself as unchangingly empathic or unchangingly nonempathic? Both of these can be traps, labeling you and cutting you off from a deeper self-awareness. If you have thought of yourself as nonempathic, try of think of one situation, any situation, in which you felt the energy from something outside yourself echoing within you. If you can recall one experience, you know that you have the ability to be empathic.

If you have thought of yourself as empathic, the rigidity of that label can affect you also. You may begin to act automatically, with less awareness. You may lose awareness of subtle differences in feelings and interactions. We all change and develop. Think of how you are more perceptive in some situations, with some people, than with others. Think of empathy as the perception of feelings, and think about how perception, like vision and touch, is a flowing, interactive response to the changes around you.

Head a page of your journal "How Thinking of Myself as Empathic or Nonempathic Has Affected Me." Write about the ways in which either of these labels has influenced your responses to others. Has either of these labels blocked your awareness?

THE IDEA OF OPPOSING POLES: MASCULINE AND FEMININE

> *In Western society men are encouraged to dread, abhor, or deny feeling weak or helpless, whereas women are encouraged to cultivate this state of being.*
>
> JEAN BAKER MILLER

> *Dualism is the ultimate lie that undermines all possibility of compassion.*
>
> MATTHEW FOX

Basic, inherently human qualities are often thought of as being either masculine or feminine. An impenetrable gulf is established between maleness and femaleness, and the essentially neutral human nature of all of us is lost in the division.

Empathy is a human ability. Perceptual abilities are not masculine or feminine. In this way of dividing qualities, however, empathy is grouped with other human characteristics as feminine. Compassion is also located at the feminine pole. In fact, a whole set of characteristics that are part of connectedness are placed at the feminine pole, while their opposing qualities of separateness are placed at the masculine pole. Thus empathy, compassion, sensitivity, dependence, emotionality, and gentleness are considered feminine, while autonomy, independence, rationality, and aggressiveness are considered masculine.

This way of thinking is confusing and harmful. The polarization of dependence and independence is a good example of the confusion. We do not seem to have a clear concept of a relationship that is a continually changing, evolving balance of these extremes. As human beings, each of us has the capacity for independence and dependence. In some situations in a relationship we want dependence, by which I mean the ability to trust and depend upon each other, and in some situations we want independence, the ability to feel good being alone with ourselves and to act alone.

Jean Baker Miller has pointed out that all of us, by virtue of being human, contain *all* human qualities. But what happens, psychologically, is that women in our culture are assigned certain qualities and then carry those qualities for both men and women. Men and women are both empathic, but women are given the role of developing and acting upon their empathic feelings. Men and women are both compassionate, but only women are allowed to show it.

If you are a woman, you may have been taught to think of

your openness to feelings as a weakness, a form of dependence in a negative sense. If you are a man, you may have been trained to hide your compassion and empathy, at first from others and then even from yourself. I hope, as you go through this book, that you will experience empathy and compassion as conditions of life, like breathing, seeing, and touching, not as good or bad, but just there, a part of our potential.

Practice 15

HOW THE IDEA OF MASCULINE AND FEMININE AS OPPOSING POLES HAS AFFECTED MY LIFE

For this practice, think about the qualities that you are expected to carry as a man or woman. Are you expected to be emotionally attuned and giving, not in a natural way that flows out of the situation, but as a role, a stereotype? Are you expected to be stoic and unemotional, not in a natural way that goes with the situation, but as a role, a stereotype? In your relationship with another person, have you divided some of the human abilities, with each of you playing opposing roles?

Head a page of your journal "How the Idea of Masculine and Feminine as Opposing Poles has Affected My Life." Let yourself express whatever feelings come to you as you think about your situation. If you feel hurt and angry, you are not alone. The division is harmful to all of us, allowing us to fully develop only half of our human abilities.

Practice 16

A UNIFYING STRUCTURE IN MY LIFE

In your journal you have written about four ideas that have affected your life. For this last practice, read the four journal entries: the isolated self, autonomy, and the opposing poles of empathic and nonempathic, masculine and femi-

nine. As you read your entries, do you see any link between them? Is there a feeling, a person, or a situation that pulls the different experiences together? Let yourself discover this unifying structure.

Head a page of your journal "A Unifying Structure in My Life." What is this structure? Write down any thoughts that come to you about the significance of this structure in your life.

In the next chapter we will look at empathy for ourselves. We will focus on self-awareness, and the practice of listening to our own feelings.

4 EMPATHY FOR YOURSELF

What you are looking for is who is looking.
ST. FRANCIS OF ASSISI

If you begin to understand what you are without trying to change it, then what you are undergoes a transformation.
JIDDU KRISHNAMURTI

Opening to oneself fully is opening to the world.
CHOGYAM TRUNGPA

PRACTICING EMPATHY IS A little like training for a team sport such as hockey. In hockey you work in harmony with the rest of the team, trying to be aware of each player's position at each moment on the ice. But first you must be able to skate well. Your body is your instrument, and you must practice being there in motion. You will not be moving in harmony with the other players if you are worrying about yourself: Am I going to stumble? Am I capable of making that shot? You have to practice until your mind and body are working as one. Then you are there, present in the motion of yourself and the others, aware of the changes that flow at each moment between you. This flowing connection is similar to empathy.

In an empathic connection, an energy flows continually between you and the other person. This energy flows in different directions. Sometimes you discover something in yourself that enables you to recognize that same thing in your friend. Sometimes you see something in your friend that startles you into seeing that same thing in yourself. Your own sadness may enable you to accept the sadness in your friend, which allows your friend to feel his sadness more safely because the two of you are together. The emotional connection between you is

37

cyclical and interactive. Because you are tuned into each other, the same thought or feeling can occur to each of you at the same time. And this interaction keeps going, because things change and we respond.

This cycle of empathy is part of our world from the beginning of our awareness. From the moment of birth, and even before birth—in the womb—we are sensing things from another person *and* sensing things inside ourselves at the same time. In order to sense anxiety in our mother we have to perceive anxiety as a sensation that has entered and become part of our own body and mind. In order to understand the anxiety we are feeling, we turn to our mother to echo that feeling. When she empathically echoes our anxiety, we can see it as real, as something substantial and acceptable. Our sensation of anxiety then becomes a human feeling, one of the many things that connects us to others and tells us that we are not *out of our mind,* not drifting someplace in outer space, all alone. We are part of the whole.

In the following practices you will focus on empathy for yourself. You will practice the perception of your own feelings. You may want to return often to the images and insights you find in these practices, because the deepening awareness of feelings is inseparable from awareness of yourself.

ALONE ON AN ISLAND

> *I am deeply convinced that gentleness, tenderness, peacefulness, and the inner freedom to move closer to one another, or to withdraw from one another, are nurtured in solitude.*
>
> HENRI NOUWEN

> *You brought me face to face with myself.*
>
> ST. AUGUSTINE

This practice is a version of the game of imagining that you are stranded on a deserted island. In traditional versions of this game you are asked to name several books you would bring with you to the island. The idea is to imagine yourself stripped of everything in your ordinary world: your job, responsibilities, entertainment, and, of course, people. You are by yourself. This is why the game has lasted so long: it gives you a chance to think about your inner world. It allows you to play with the idea of solitude, and the freedom to be yourself. Then, alone on your island, the books you choose reflect the nature of your inner self: not the part of you that reads to get a better job or to get along with other people, but the part of you that reads to affirm the truth of yourself.

Practice 17

ALONE ON MY ISLAND

Close your eyes, take a deep breath, and feel the tension leaving your body with the breath. Breathe quietly, focusing your attention on the rhythm of your breathing. Take another deep breath and let the tension flow out of your body with the breath.

Imagine yourself on a beautiful island. It is a perfect island for you. You are physically and mentally comfortable and at peace. This is your island, your world.

Now, think about how your body feels on your island. Think about how your mind feels. What is the sense of connection between your body and your mind, alone on your island? Where are you in relation to the water and the land? You can move around if you want; you can swim, float on the water, float over the ground, or sit quietly. Sense the connection between you and the ground, the water, and the air around you.

Head a page of your journal "Alone on My Island." Write down answers to the following questions. Write whatever comes to you. The answers can be brief and you can leave any question blank. You will return to this practice later and can add more details.

1. *How does my body feel?*
2. *How does my mind feel?*
3. *What is the connection between my body and mind?*
4. *How am I moving?*
5. *What is the connection between me and the ground, the water, and the air around me?*

WITH OTHERS ON MY ISLAND

Being alone on your island is getting in touch with your inner self. It is the beginning of empathy for yourself. In the next few practices you are going to compare the sense of being alone with the sense of being with someone else. You are going to imagine different people joining you on the island, much as you might imagine taking along different books in the game. You will feel different things inside yourself when these people join you. It is these intuitive feelings that you want to focus upon in the next practices.

Practice 18

WITH A CHILD ON MY ISLAND

Repeat the beginning of Practice 17, in which you took a deep breath, relaxed, and imagined yourself alone on your island. This feeling of being at peace with yourself and your surroundings is the central feeling to which you want to return. It is the feeling of being centered.

Now imagine that a child joins you on your island. It can be any child. Close your eyes, relax, and let the image of a child appear on the island. Concentrate upon how you feel as the child joins you. Is there any change in your body? Is there any change in your mind? Sense the kind of connection you feel between you and the child. Try moving around with the child. Do you and the child seem to be moving in harmony or in opposition to each other? Sense how you feel with the child.

Head a page of your journal "With a Child on My Is-land." Answer some or all of the following questions. Re-member that the important thing here is your empathic perception of your own feelings. For some people the pres-ence of a child can create the feeling of being more com-fortable, more centered, a wanted anchor. For others, the presence of a child can bring tension and discomfort, an unwanted anchor. And some people do not feel any change; they are the same, alone and with the child. The purpose of this practice is to get in touch with your own feelings.

1. *How does my body feel?*
2. *How does my mind feel?*
3. *What is the connection between my body and mind?*
4. *How do I move with the child?*
5. *What is the connection between me and the child?*

Practice 19

WITH A WOMAN ON MY ISLAND

Imagine yourself, again, alone on your island. Play with the sense of being yourself, completely comfortable and at peace with your surroundings. Let that feeling develop, to-gether with any details that come into your mind.

You might, for example, imagine the place where you live on the island. It can be a house, a tree-house, or any kind of a structure you want. You can imagine flowers, a musical instrument, even a computer, in your dwelling. This is your island; if you want a computer, imagine it there and it will be there.

Now imagine that a woman, any woman you choose, joins you on your island. Focus upon your feelings as she is there with you. Are there any changes in the way that your body feels? Are there any changes in your mind? What kind of changes are they? Move around with her, dancing or floating or whatever kind of motion comes naturally to you. Feel the connection between yourself and the woman.

Return to the page in your journal titled "Alone on My Island." Add any of the new details that you imagined about your dwelling on the island.

Now, head a new page of your journal "With a Woman on My Island." Recall any changes you sensed when the woman joined you on the island. Answer the following questions based on your perception of these changes. If there were no changes, record that, for that too is an insight.

1. How does my body feel?
2. How does my mind feel?
3. What is the connection between my body and mind?
4. How do I move with the woman?
5. What is the connection between me and the woman?

Practice 20

WITH A MAN ON MY ISLAND

The purpose of each practice in this set is to tune into your feelings, to develop the skill of empathy for yourself. You may feel peaceful alone, and then lose some of that centered feeling when you are joined by another person. You may feel uneasy, even frightened, alone, and then feel secure and happy when joined by another person. Notice whatever feelings come to you.

Imagine yourself alone on your island. Again, imagine the details of your island: the landscape, the dwelling, and the objects you want to have with you. You might want wild animals around you, birds in the trees and porpoises in the ocean. You might want a dog.

Now imagine that a man, any man, joins you on your

island. *Imagine the changes, if any, in your body and in your mind. Feel the connection between your body and mind with the man on the island. Move around with him, and sense the kind of connection you have together, moving in harmony or in some kind of opposition. Sense the connection between you and the man.*

Return again to your journal entry "Alone on My Island." Add any details about your island that came to you in this last practice.

Head another page of your journal "With a Man on My Island" and answer these questions.

1. *How does my body feel?*
2. *How does my mind feel?*
3. *What is the connection between my body and mind?*
4. *How do I move with the man?*
5. *What is the connection between me and the man?*

Practice 21

EMPATHY FOR MYSELF ON MY ISLAND

You have written four journal entries about yourself on your island. For this practice, go back and read each of the entries, noting your basic feelings. As you read, see if there is one insight about yourself that emerges from your feelings.

Head a page of your journal "Empathy for Myself on My Island." Write down that one insight, that thing you found in reading your entries. The island you have created is a place where you can be yourself. It is a place where you are centered. You might find that you lose the sense of being yourself with some people but not with others. You might find that you feel most centered when you are with a certain person. You might discover that you feel best outdoors, and you don't want a house on your island.

Write down whatever comes to you, even if it seems

strange. It probably expresses something significant about part of yourself. If it seems strange, it is because it is a new thought, something which will take time to integrate into your knowledge of yourself. In developing awareness of feelings, it helps to hold on to them, to capture them somehow, and we try to capture them by putting them into words. It is a little like putting a butterfly in a cage; it is not the same moving, fluid creature. In most cases, it is not the feelings that are strange, but their expression in words. The feelings have always been with you, moving and fluid. The skill of empathy is the skill of bringing those feelings to awareness.

TUNING INTO OURSELVES

At the innermost core of all loneliness is a deep and powerful yearning for union with one's lost self.

BRENDAN FRANCIS

Tuning into our own emotions is sometimes as easy as feeling the wind on our face. We simply sense the touch. But sometimes we block our awareness of the inner or outer world. We can be unaware of the wind blowing on our face. And it can be difficult to tune into a feeling.

When we are with another person there are many reasons why we might not pick up an emotion: it is *her* emotion, and she may want to hide it. We may not know her well enough to recognize what, for her, are significant signs of sadness. And sometimes, our attention is focused on other aspects of the situation and we miss the emotional meaning.

But with our own feelings the contact is so pure and direct, it is hard to understand how confusion is even possible. It is *our* happiness, *our* sorrow. How could we not be tuned in? Why would we hide our feelings from ourselves?

Our minds are incredibly complex, and the connection between a physical sensation and our mental awareness is like the connection between two friends. It is a cycle which constantly responds to the total situation, within and around us. There is a delicate interdependence between feelings and awareness.

Take a situation of physical pain. Imagine that you are a hockey player or a figure skater during a crucial competition. All of you—your mind, body, and emotions, together with the expectations of everyone around you—wants you to perform. Then you hurt your ankle seriously. But you only have to skate for a short time to complete the event, and you want to do this more than anything else. What happens? Your mind shuts off the pain. The signals coming from your ankle, which tell your mind that you are injured and allow you to feel the pain, are simply cut off. Your ankle is still hurt, but you feel no pain. You continue your performance.

There are many stories of soldiers in combat, mothers rescuing children, and athletes in competition, who were seriously injured but felt no pain until whatever they had to do was over. This blocking of feeling is a basic survival mechanism of the human and animal mind. Ronald Melzack and Patrick Wall, who did a great deal of the research on how we block out pain, called it *the gate theory*. When we need to, we close the gate. If our mind can close off the searing pain of a twisted ankle, it can easily close off the delicate emotions of sadness or well-being.

Why would we want to close off awareness of our emotions? Unfortunately, it is easier for us to conform to the ordinary world if we stop feeling. Conforming is performing—but only in the context of social conventions. Conforming is acting happy at a party, acting professionally at a business meeting, acting sad at a funeral. If it happens that we feel despair at a party, fear during a business meeting, or happiness at a funeral, we have trained ourselves to hide these deviant emotions. And a lifetime of training, together with the enormous pressures put upon us to conform, makes it easier for us to simply block the feelings. Sometimes, during the party, we feel the despair and as quickly as possible push it down, away, out of our awareness. Many other times, far too often, we do not allow ourselves to feel it at all. We close the gate. There may be a small sense of discomfort, and that is all. Later, we may realize that the sense of discomfort was a tiny opening to the real feeling.

TOUCHSTONES

> *The great cave of memory, and I know not what hidden and inexpressible recesses within it, takes in all these things to be called up and brought forth when there is need for them.*
>
> ST. AUGUSTINE

> *It is all right to copy what you see, but it is much better to draw what you can no longer see except through your memory. This is a transformation in which imagination collaborates with memory. All you reproduce is what struck you.*
>
> EDGAR DEGAS

To increase awareness of certain feelings, we are going to use what Matthew Arnold called *touchstones*. A touchstone is an intuitively clear, strong example of some kind of experience. In research on the structure of the mind, Michael Posner and Eleanor Rosch found that we group similar experiences around a central, prototypical example of that experience.

Imagine, for a moment, this experience: I saw a bird this morning. What kind of bird did you see in your mind? You probably saw a robin or a sparrow, not a pelican or a vulture. We group our experiences of birds around a clear example, and a small, familiar bird like a robin captures the essence of birdness for most of us. Similarly, we group our experiences of an emotion around a clear example of that emotion. Your touchstone for a feeling is an experience that captures, for you, the essence of that feeling.

Identifying a touchstone will help you focus upon that feeling. Imagine that you have a touchstone for feeling peaceful with another person. It might be a memory, for example, of a day you climbed in the mountains with a friend and both of you felt perfectly tuned to each other and the surrounding world. Now, when you are with different people in different situations, you feel more or less peaceful. Your touchstone is a way of tuning into the peacefulness of the present moment. It helps you recognize the feeling.

Touchstones for feelings are powerful memories. They are not necessarily major events in your external life, although sometimes they are. They also can be small, subtle moments of unusual awareness. But they stay with you. When you remember them, they return with a vividness of sensory detail that brings them right into the present with you.

Touchstones can be significant events in your inner world. You glimpsed something—inner peace, unity with another person, a sense of yourself—that took you out of the ordinary way of being and into a different sense of reality. You held onto this knowledge.

You can return to this knowledge whenever you need it. You can use your touchstones to guide your inner journey.

The next two practices will help you to identify two touchstones: your touchstone for feeling upset and your touchstone for feeling peaceful. These are quiet, subtle feelings. They do not shout out their presence, like excitement or fear. They are feelings that often occur in the presence of another person. And, because of the complexities of our relationships, they are feelings that we sometimes push out of awareness. Identifying the touchstones will bring the feelings into focus.

Practice 22

My Touchstone for Feeling Upset

Think of several different experiences of feeling upset. Let your mind wander over different times in your life, in different situations with different people, when you were upset.

Settle on one experience in which your feeling of being upset was especially clear. When you remember it now, you can feel the sensation. Focus on that experience. This will be your touchstone.

Head a page of your journal "My Touchstone for Feeling Upset." Describe the experience in detail. Write as clearly as you can about the actual bodily feeling of being upset.

Think for a few moments about two or three of the other experiences you remembered of feeling upset. Then head a page of your journal "Times When I Feel Upset." Write down any insight that occurs to you as you think of these experiences as a group. Is there any pattern in the different experiences? Is there a particular kind of situation in which you feel upset? Are certain people usually involved?

The next time you feel slightly uncomfortable, as if something is wrong, think of your touchstone for feeling upset. See if your present feeling fits your touchstone in any way. Recalling your touchstone can help you stay aware of your present feeling.

Practice 23

MY TOUCHSTONE FOR FEELING PEACEFUL

Recall three or four times when you felt peaceful. Relax and let yourself relive these experiences. Choose the experience which is closest for you to the essence of being at peace. That experience will be your touchstone.

Head a page of your journal "My Touchstone for Feeling Peaceful." Describe the details of the experience, and the essence of feeling peaceful.

Think again about the several times when you felt peaceful. Is there a structure that unifies these experiences? Are you alone or with another person? Do you feel especially connected to the world around you? Head a page of your journal *"Times When I Feel Peaceful." Write down any in-sight about the experiences. Describe your sense of your-self and the world around you during these experiences.*

You can consciously seek peacefulness by seeking situa-tions which are similar to your touchstone experience. You can slowly increase the times you feel peaceful in your life. You can go to a special place, be with a special person, or do whatever brings you a sense of peace. Being aware of your touchstone will help you find that peacefulness again. As the final part of this practice, create now, at this moment, a situation in which you feel peaceful.

TUNING INTO YOUR BODY

I had placed myself behind my own back, refusing to see myself.
ST. AUGUSTINE

The difficulty is to learn to perceive with your whole body, not with just your eyes and reason.
CARLOS CASTANEDA

The feeling of being disconnected from yourself is very close to the feeling of being sick. You feel as if you are lost in a fog. The fog is within as well as around you. Everything is con-fusing. Your place in the universe is not clear. Your own feel-ings are hazy. You lose your balance, lose track of time, and wake up not knowing where you are. You do not have a clear sense of yourself.

When you are physically ill, your body is occupied with the potentially life-or-death task of becoming well again. When animals get sick, they normally go to a safe place, curl up, and wait out the illness. They remove themselves from awareness of the outside world by hiding, and from awareness of them-selves by sleeping. All of their physical and mental strength works toward healing the body's wound.

Our lives are not as simple as animal lives, and our minds sometimes work against our bodies in complex ways. But when we are sick, much of our energy is directed toward fighting the illness, whether our mind consciously wants this or not. The body is designed to try to survive, to go on living. When we are sick, the body does its best to avoid experiences that will drain its energy. This means avoiding externally created dangers, such as extreme cold or heat, and reducing internally created dangers, such as stressful thoughts and feelings. So when we are sick we close off awareness: like animals, we focus on healing.

When your body is strong and healthy, the fog lifts. You feel alive, and your sense of yourself is clear. Your motions are in balance. You are aware of the air around you. You are open to feelings.

In the next two practices, you will recall the feeling of sickness and the feeling of health, your body at its best. The two extreme conditions of your body are dramatic examples of potential changes in awareness. In sickness, you close off almost everything. When your body is at its best, you can be fully aware.

Practice 24

My Body in Illness

The purpose of this practice is to become more conscious of what it is like to close off awareness. It may sound paradoxical to become aware of not being aware. But it is possible, because a part of us is aware of our unawareness. In our amazing complexity, we can look at ourselves from inside and out at the same time.

Remember a time when you were very sick. Think of the way you felt, the particular sensations. Was there a fogginess, a sense of not being able to think or feel clearly? Was there a desire to retreat from everything? Relive the bodily sensations of being sick.

Head a page of your journal "My Body in Sickness." Write about the situation, including whatever comes back to you: the cause of the illness, the room you were in, the bed, the position of your body. List the sensations as you remember them. Then write about the connection between yourself and the space around you. Did the space seem unclear or foggy? Did you feel disconnected from the world, withdrawn into yourself? Describe that feeling.

Practice 25

MY BODY AT ITS BEST

Think of the times when your body feels at its best. It might be during exercise, when you feel energy and strength. It might be after exercise, when you feel a sense of physical peace. When does your body feel at its best?

How does your body feel at these times? Focus on the bodily sensations. What are the physical feelings? Now focus on your inner state. Are you feeling especially open and free? Are you feeling especially gentle, powerful, or both? What is the relationship between your body and the space around you? Relive that feeling of your body at its best.

Head a page of your journal "My Body at Its Best." Write down the bodily sensations, and your feelings. Write down, also, the sense of your body in the space around it. Do you feel an energy connecting you with the space around you? Do you feel a calmness within and around you? Do you have an unusually clear sense of yourself?

You can use your sense of yourself in these two practices as guides to awareness. If you begin to feel that sense of fogginess, you know that you are closing yourself off. You may be getting sick. Or you may be withdrawing from a difficult situation. Stay open to whatever is happening inside you. When you are sick, you wait for your body to heal. When you are closing off feelings, wait patiently for the fog to lift.

In the next chapter we will look at our connection to children. Empathic awareness seems to occur naturally in the presence of a child. We will look at the things about children that make empathy so natural for us.

5 COMPASSION AND EMPATHY FOR CHILDREN

Almost imperceptibly, a newborn baby's body moves in rhythm to its mother's voice, performing a kind of dance as the mother continues talking.

MARSHALL AND PHYLLIS KLAUS

Suffer little children, and forbid them not, to come unto me: for of such is the kingdom of heaven.

JESUS

He who is in harmony with the Tao
is like a newborn child.

LAO TZU

A CHILD IS OPEN TO FEELINGS. The ways of thinking that close adults to compassion and empathy are not formed yet. Infants seem to be naturally empathic.

A recent psychological discovery tells us about the subtle nature of the infant's response to human interactions. William Condon has studied infants responding to their mothers from the first moments of birth. In slow-motion films we can see the baby moving in synchrony with the rhythm of the mother's body and voice: they seem to be swaying together, like trees in the wind.

The baby is responding to a subtle, delicate aspect of an interaction, its rhythmic structure. The baby's perception of the rhythmic structure is the beginning of the perception of feelings. This is not to say, of course, that the baby can consciously recognize different emotions. The baby does not think "Oh yes, mother is anxious today." It is that the baby echoes a basic rhythm which is more or less calm, more or less agitated. As the baby responds, the mother responds, echoing the baby's motion. And this cycle of responsiveness and openness continues, with each tuned to the other's rhythm. This tuning to rhythm is the basis of empathy.

You may have heard people say that young children are not empathic. They mean that young children cannot consciously, mentally, put themselves in someone else's situation—they cannot, for example, *think* themselves into their mother's position in life and remain quiet because they know she needs to get work done.

Mental understanding is an important aspect of the whole experience of adult empathy: we think and feel in an integrated way. But the basis of the empathic feeling itself is a bodily response, a tuning-in to an emotional rhythm. The child is able to tune in from birth, and responds to a rhythm that is more or less peaceful, more or less agitated. Later, the child develops the mental ability to give conscious meaning to that rhythmic structure. A young child is amazingly empathic, if we think of empathy as a natural, perceptual response.

Practice 26

A CHILDHOOD MEMORY OF EMPATHY

Recall a memory from childhood in which you felt that someone was upset, or that something was happening that you did not understand. This happens most often with our parents, who think they can spare us suffering by hiding their emotions. They succeed only in hiding the reason for the emotion, not the emotion itself. As children we pick up the vibrations without understanding the situation; we just sense something.

Recall a time when you sensed that someone was upset and you didn't know why. A relative may have been sick; a parent may have left home. It may be that now you understand the situation, or at least part of it. Try to relive the experience of just sensing that something is happening. This is an early experience of empathy.

Head a page of your journal "A Childhood Memory of Empathy." Write down all of the details you remember about the event. Describe your feelings then, as you remember them.

OUR NATURAL EMPATHY FOR CHILDREN

> *One of the newborn's first responses is to move into a quiet, but alert state of consciousness. The baby is still; his body molds to yours; his hands touch your skin; his eyes open wide and are bright and shiny. He looks directly at you.*
>
> MARSHALL AND PHYLLIS KLAUS

Although we normally do not *see* the rhythmic connection between a child and ourselves, we can feel it. Everyone who has walked a baby to sleep in the middle of the night has felt it— the mutual calming and quieting of the heart rate and breathing of both of you.

Why does empathy for a child seem to occur so naturally for us? There are several answers, and we will look at each of them. Each represents a special element in our relationship with a child.

EMPATHY FOR A CHILD: TRUST

> *Can you let your body become supple as a newborn child's?*
>
> LAO TZU

A child who has been cared for and protected is naturally trusting. This trust includes openness to feelings. The child receives our feelings just as the child receives our physical touch. And we can respond to a child's openness by being more open ourselves. We sense the trust and respond by trusting.

Our trust enables us to be freer, more ourselves, with a child. Even adults who seem terribly serious and sedate have been known to get down on their hands and knees and crawl around with a child, grunting and squealing. Others who are chronically impatient and cannot tolerate *wasting time* find themselves waiting peacefully while a child slowly ties her shoe. They trust that the child will not laugh at them as they crawl on the floor. They trust that if they let certain parts of themselves show, like the quiet, patient part, the child will not use this against them. Empathy grows naturally and easily in the safety of mutual trust.

Practice 27

LETTING YOURSELF BE FREE WITH A CHILD

Recall a time when you were with a child and felt some-thing you normally do not feel. You expressed some part of yourself that you usually keep hidden. You were free to be yourself with the child.

Head a page of your journal "Letting Myself Be Free With a Child." Describe your experience with the child. What did you do that was unusual for you? How were you feeling about the child? How did you feel about yourself?

EMPATHY FOR A CHILD: SURVIVAL

> *Wholeheartedness of concentration means that all our faculties come into play: conscious reasoning, intuition, feelings, percep-tion, curiosity, liking, sympathy, wanting to help, or whatever.*
> KAREN HORNEY

Empathy is part of a child's survival. There are many ways in which we as adults can know that something is wrong with a young child. We can see, hear, touch, taste, and smell danger. But sometimes these signals are unclear, or absent. Instinct tells us that our best chance of keeping a child safe is to open ourselves to all aspects of the situation, including the perception of the child's feelings. Karen Horney called this special attentiveness *wholeheartedness of concentration.*

There are many stories of mothers and fathers who have sensed that something is wrong, have trusted that feeling, and have rushed their child to the hospital just in time to prevent the child's death. In some cases a doctor has examined the child just hours before the crisis and has told the parent that nothing is wrong. But the parent *knows,* empathically, that something is wrong. The parent senses something coming from inside the child.

A mother left her young child with a lifeguard at a pool. It was a private pool, with only a few children for the lifeguard to watch, and it had always been safe. The mother was changing in the locker room when a feeling of panic swept over her. She ran out to the pool to find her child being pulled out of the water by the club manager. The lifeguard had gone away for a minute and the child had wandered down to the deep end and fallen in. The manager had been looking out of his office window, saw the child fall, and ran out to save her.

The mother's feeling needs to be understood. Out of sight, out of hearing, and out of reach, she was not receiving any of the usual perceptual information from the child. Some people dismiss the mother's panic as an odd coincidence. Others say that later, in reliving the event, the mother only *thinks* she remembers a feeling of panic before she actually saw the danger. Although there is no scientific evidence for this theory, it is just as possible that the child was communicating extreme fear to her mother at the moment she fell into the pool. The mother felt panic because she was receiving the energy of the child's fear.

This kind of empathic communication is unusual, but it is important in understanding the potential power of empathy. In the case of a child, we are very aware of the child's dependence upon us. We are aware, at the most basic level of survival, of our *connection.* In other relationships, it is possible to remain unaware of connection, to quietly close ourselves off to the energy of feelings. With a child, if we close off our awareness some crisis brings us right back to the present moment, and the reality of our connection.

EMPATHY FOR A CHILD: DEPENDENCE

> *I do not love him because he is good, but because he is my little child.*
>
> RABINDRANATH TAGORE

In our society dependence implies weakness and vulnerability. It means we have failed to become that isolated self that our culture demands. In recent writings on relationships involving alcoholism, the term *codependency* is used to describe a negative relationship.

But the interdependence of child and adult, and the interdependence of all living things, can be experienced as the deepest harmony, the finding of the self in true freedom and peace. This requires a different understanding of dependence, and the *co* (or mutual) dependence that connects us. We have to look at dependence from another framework: the sacredness of trust.

Because a child is so vulnerable, and the child's dependence is at such a deep level, we do everything we can to protect and to care for the trust. This trust can lead to a relationship that is incredibly comforting and secure. Many parents say that the closest bond they ever felt was with their child.

In the framework of trust, dependence is a freeing connection. The conventional opposition between dependence and independence doesn't make sense anymore. In order for a child to know independence, the child must be able to trust the adult. In order to know independence, the child must be able to be *dependent*. And the adult depends upon the child too. In order to develop a close, secure bond with a child, the adult needs to sense that the child is trusting. The adult depends on the child's trust. The connection between the adult and child is an ever-changing, delicate balance. Dependence and independence are shared between them.

Practice 28

THE DEPENDENCE OF A CHILD

In this practice, think about the dependence of a child. Let whatever you feel and think happen, whether the thoughts and feelings are positive, negative, or both. This is a difficult subject; try to stay open to all your feelings.

Head a page of your journal "How I Feel About the Dependence of a Child." Write down your thoughts and feelings.

Practice 29

TRUST WITH A CHILD

This practice involves spending an hour or two with a child. It could be your own child, or a child whom you know well. But you might also want to try this practice with a child you have just met.

Go to a place where both you and the child will feel comfortable and safe. Watch the child, and follow the child's lead. Let the child decide what the two of you will do together.

Remain empathically open to the child's feelings. Do you sense an openness and feeling of trust coming from the child? Young children are sometimes anxious about being away from their parents, and you may sense this anxiety. If the child is anxious, stay empathically open to the feeling. Be there for the child.

As you play, or sit quietly, focus on the things that you and the child are doing together. Are you doing anything that you would not normally do with an adult? Are you sitting on the floor? Are you more comfortable with the silence? Are you more patient with the time? Are you feeling or acting in any way that is unusual for you?

Head a page of your journal "Trust with a Child." Describe the time you spent together. Did you act differently in any way with the child? Was there some quality in you that you were able to express more easily with the child? Did you feel a sense of trust from the child? Did you feel that you trusted the child?

Practice 30

HOLDING AN INFANT

This practice asks you, if possible, to hold an infant. Perhaps you can hold an infant who is known to you through friends or family. If not, there are many infants in hospitals who need human touch desperately. If you want to, you can volunteer to spend time with these infants.

Look at the infant. How does the infant respond to you? Does it look into your eyes? Place your finger in the infant's hand. Does it clasp your finger? Hold the infant. What are you feeling? Is the infant communicating with you through touch? Notice everything that you are feeling as you hold the infant.

Head a page of your journal "Holding an Infant." Describe the ways that you felt connected to the infant. Did you feel the infant's need for you at that moment? How did you feel about the infant's dependence on you?

Although doing this practice will take some time and effort, especially if you have to go through hospital procedures, it will be worth it. The connection between an infant and an adult is quite amazing. If you can feel this connection, you will learn a great deal about the nature of empathy, and the reality of dependence. And you will be helping an infant simply by being there, giving empathy and touch.

EMPATHY FOR A CHILD:
ATTENTION TO FEELINGS

When you believe your baby is responding to you, you actually are in tune with each other. Your baby's body is prepared for a conversation with you long before he or she can say the words.
MARSHALL AND PHYLLIS KLAUS

It doesn't matter what you say to a plant. You can just as well make up words; what's important is the feeling of liking it, and treating it as an equal.
CARLOS CASTANEDA

A very young child is predominantly nonverbal. Sounds, the motion of the body, and touch, are possible ways for the child to communicate. Because we are not expecting verbal communication from the child, we open ourselves most fully to the nonverbal modes. We listen to the tone and rhythm of the sounds rather than to the verbal meaning. We see and feel the rhythms of the child's body in breathing, sleeping, crawling, and walking. We feel the nature of the child's touch. In attending to these nonverbal modes, we are naturally attuned to feelings. We are being empathic.

When we give our attention to the child, we are not expecting anything in particular. We are not thinking "The child is going to expect me to dress up today," or "The child is going to be leaving for work in an hour." Free of these expectations and worries about what is going to happen, we can really sense from moment to moment what *is* happening between ourselves and the child. Freud called this *evenly hovering attention*. We do not select certain things and block out others; we open our minds to everything, evenly and with quiet attention. We are there in the moment.

Being there in the moment is essential to empathy. If the child is peaceful, we will feel it. If the child becomes disturbed, we will feel it. We sense what is happening right there, and we sense any change. In attending to the moment, we are empathically attuned.

Practice 31

BEING THERE WITH A CHILD

Arrange to spend some time alone with a young child who knows you fairly well. Go to a place where both of you will feel safe, perhaps the child's room. Get down on the floor with the child and see the room from the child's viewpoint. Stay quiet and let the child lead you. If the child is playing with blocks, try to sense the blocks the way the child does. Don't try to teach the child anything by stacking or arranging the blocks in some preconceived way. Don't talk.

Feel what it is like to be there with the child, sensing whatever the child is sensing at that moment. You will probably find adult thoughts drifting into your mind: "I have to make supper soon," or "That meeting tomorrow is going to be awful." Whenever that happens, just gently bring yourself back to being there with the child. Give your wholehearted attention to the reality of the child.

Head a page of your journal "Being There with a Child." Describe the kind of attention you experienced in being with the child.

Practice 32

VISUAL ATTENTION

This practice is fun and can give interesting insights into visual understanding. Turn on the television without the sound. You can use any program, but a good one to practice with is the evening news. Watch the news anchor talking into the camera, and the two or three co-anchors talking to each other. Focus your attention on how they are feeling from moment to moment. See how much you can pick up about their feelings by watching their faces and body motions.

Head a page of your journal "Visual Attention." De-

scribe what you saw. Did they seem to be tense at all, or more tense at one point than another? What did their smiles feel like? Was there a difference in the way they smiled when they faced the camera or faced each other?

Whatever you pick up from this practice is interesting, because you are sensing emotions from the changes of the face, hands, and upper body. When the sound is on as usual, your attention is divided between the meaning of the words and the visual meaning. With the sound off, you can calmly focus on the visual, nonverbal meaning. If you enjoy this practice, do it regularly; each time you can discover something about your own visual perception.

COMPASSION FOR CHILDREN

> *The child and I are one: no one pities; no one asks for help; no one helps.*
>
> THICH NHAT HANH

> *All have the same sorrows, the same joys as I, and I must guard them like myself.*
>
> SHANTIDEVA

There is something intolerable to all of us about the suffering of children. In the Vietnam War, it was the suffering and deaths of Vietnamese children that changed the minds of many Americans about the rightness of the war. On television we see so much suffering and violence, in this country and all over the world, that many of us have closed off our feelings. Yet the picture of a starving infant, or of a little girl hit by a bullet as she is playing in front of her house, still penetrates our armor. We feel compassion. We feel the suffering, and we feel the need to do something about it. We want to save our children. And by *our*, we do not mean our own family, or our country, or our religion: we mean all human children. This is universal compassion.

Practice 33

COMPASSION FOR AN UNKNOWN CHILD

In this practice try to recall a moment when you felt compassion for a child who was unknown to you. You may have seen the child on the street. You may have seen a picture of the child. Remember the incident and your feelings.

Head a page of your journal "Compassion for an Unknown Child." Describe the incident and your feelings. What was the nature of the connection between you? Did you feel something within you as an actual sensation? Did you want to do something to help? If you were unable to really help, how did you feel about that?

THE BETRAYAL OF TRUST

> *In the face of suffering, one has no right to turn away, not to see.*
> ELIE WIESEL

> *Children help you remember how small and helpless you actually were.*
> ELLEN BASS AND LAURA DAVIS

All of our connections to a child that make empathy so natural also lead to compassion. When a child is suffering, we know that the child needs us and we want to help.

There is another component in our compassion for children: our sense of their innocence. A child who is starving did not contribute to a society in which some people have five houses and others have no house and no food. A child with cancer did not create a world of illness. We see these children and there is no way to explain their suffering. And because it is so clear that they are innocent, that some awful thing about our world has fastened onto them and is destroying them, we feel responsible. We feel the sacredness of trust. They trusted that they would at least have the chance to grow up, and their trust was betrayed. We feel angry.

Practice 34

A BETRAYAL OF MY TRUST AS A CHILD

For this practice, return to the feeling of being a child, being innocent, and having your trust betrayed. It can be any kind of event, any kind of wrong. Recall the experience. As you relive it, the feeling of betrayal will be powerfully present. It will seem to be happening again right now. It is, of course, happening in your inner world.

Head a page of your journal "A Betrayal of my Trust as a Child." Write about the event, including the details. Describe your feelings as a child. Now, as an adult thinking back, do you feel anger, sadness, or any other feeling? Do you feel compassion for the child who was yourself?

Practice 35

COMPASSION FOR A CHILD I KNOW

Recall an experience of feeling compassion for a child you know. Relax and allow different experiences with children to drift through your mind. When you feel ready, focus on one of them. It may be a memory that came to you during one of the other practices in this chapter.

Relive the experience with the child. Recall the situation, the adults involved, their roles and your role in the situation, and the child's suffering. Let all of the complexities of the situation arise in your mind. Relive your feelings.

Head a page of your journal "Compassion for a Child I Know." Describe the situation: who was there, the nature of the child's suffering, and the possible causes. Describe your own feelings. Did you want to help? Were you able to help? Can you feel now the strength of your own compassion for the child?

We feel empathy and compassion naturally for a child. The connection can be more difficult with a friend. When two adults are involved, cultural ideas are more likely to block our feelings. Yet a friend is someone we have chosen, someone to whom we respond in an important way. In the next chapter we will look at that response, and the ways that compassion and empathy are part of friendship.

6 COMPASSION AND EMPATHY FOR FRIENDS

Home is not where you live but where they understand you.
CHRISTIAN MORGENSTERN

Making contact involves two people at a time and three parts. Each person in contact with himself or herself and each in contact with the other.
VIRGINIA SATIR

Kindness is more important than wisdom, and the recognition of this is the beginning of wisdom.
THEODORE RUBIN

*F*RIENDSHIP MEANS DIFFERENT THINGS to each of us, and we each have different kinds of friends. First, we will look at some of the typical ideas of friendship, and you can think about whether they fit your own concept. In the first set of practices, you will develop your *own* definition of a friend. As your definition evolves, we will explore the importance of compassion and empathy in friendships.

FRIENDSHIP

You can be yourself with a friend. This is an essential quality of friendship for most people. If this is missing, the person can still be important in other ways, as a teacher for example, but not as a friend.

You can talk to a friend, but not necessarily about all things.

You can have a friend with whom you go fishing, without ever feeling the need to talk.

You laugh together at the same things. And you feel comfortable enough to laugh at yourself when you are together.

You have known each other for a long time. Because you know something about each other's past, a lot of things do not need elaboration or explanation. There is less chance of misunderstandings with an old friend.

For some people, a friend must be there whenever there is difficulty or need. This is not a requirement for everyone. Some people have close friends who disappear from their lives for a long time, without any feelings of anger or abandonment. One day one of them will call, and the feeling is the same as it always was between them.

The concept of a friend is fluid, and friendships can be as different as the people involved. The important thing is to think about your own feelings toward friends.

Practice 36

MY DEFINITION OF A FRIEND

The purpose of this practice is to develop your own definition of a friend. Think for a while about what is important to you in a friend. You may come up with only one or two items or a long list. Think about the importance of each quality in your friendships.

Head a page of your journal "My Definition of a Friend." Describe the qualities that are important to you. Is one of the qualities most important to you?

Practice 37

MY FRIENDS

Focus on your actual friends. You may have a relatively long list, including friends you have not seen for several years; or you may have a short list, perhaps only one person

you can really count on to be there for you. The number of
people you think of as friends will depend upon your definition of friendship.

Divide a page of your journal into three columns. Label
column one *"My Friends"* and list your friends.

Practice 38

QUALITIES

*Think slowly about each of your friends on the list. Turn
back to the qualities you described in your definition of a
friend. Which of these qualities does each friend have? It is
possible that one friend may have all of the qualities and
one may have none. Probably the strength of the quality
will be different for each friend.*

*Label column two "Qualities." For every friend, note if
that person has each quality which is part of your definition.*

Practice 39

THE SIGNIFICANCE OF THE QUALITY
FOR THE FRIENDSHIP

*The purpose of this practice is to shift the focus from a de-
scription of your friend or yourself to the nature of the
connection between you. For example, assume that you
listed "sense of humor" as an important quality in a
friend. When you did this, the focus was on your friend.
Now, shift the focus to the* connection between *you.
What is the significance of a sense of humor in this friendship? Why does it matter? It could be that you feel really
good when you are laughing together. It could be that you
feel most connected to each other when you are both laughing. It could be that you see things more clearly through
your friend's humor.*

Label column three "The Significance of the Quality for the Friendship." Describe the significance of each quality for each friendship.

Practice 40

WHAT A FRIEND MEANS TO ME

Read across the three columns: my friends, their qualities, and the significance of their qualities for the friendship. At this point you may have lines and arrows criss-crossing across the page. With real friends in living relationships neat little rows and columns never quite work. But there is probably some creative insight woven into the structure you have made. What does a friend mean to you?

Head a new page of your journal "What a Friend Means to Me." Write about any insight you found in your row and column structure.

THE ROLE OF COMPASSION AND EMPATHY IN THE QUALITIES OF FRIENDSHIP

> . . . *Man can no more survive psychologically in a psychological milieu that does not respond empathically to him than he can survive physically in an atmosphere that contains no oxygen.*
>
> HEINZ KOHUT

> *What happens to another, whether it be a joy or a sorrow, happens to you.*
>
> MEISTER ECKHART

If you look at the things that are important to you in a friendship, you will find that compassion and empathy are intricately involved. If you are able to be yourself with a friend, for example, it means that your friend is open to all the different parts of you. If you want to laugh at a funeral, your friend accepts your feeling. If you are in trouble, your friend does not turn away.

Practice 41

EMPATHY IN A DIFFICULT SITUATION

In this practice, think about one friend who has the quality that is most important to you in a friendship. Imagine facing a difficult situation together with this friend. Imagine the scene, the two of you together, and the difficult situation. How does your friend's presence help you?

Let me use sense of humor *again as an example. Imagine that one of you says something funny about the problem, and you both laugh. What are you feeling? What is your friend feeling? Is there a sense that you are both feeling the same thing? Is there an empathic connection? If there is, does this connection help you through the difficulty?*

Head a page of your journal "Empathy in a Difficult Situation." Describe your friend, the situation, and the way you approach it together. Describe the quality of the friendship that helps you through the difficulty.

Practice 42

EMPATHY IN MY FRIENDSHIPS

For this practice, think about your friends and the qualities that are important to each friendship. Think of the two of you together, doing whatever you normally do. Are you both feeling the same thing at the same time? Think about peaceful and happy situations in addition to difficult ones. Are you in tune with each other? Are you open to each other's feelings?

Head a page of your journal "Empathy in My Friend-ships." Describe your different friendships. How is em-pathy part of your friendships?

A GAP IN A FRIENDSHIP

A friend is not always there for you, and you are not always there for a friend. When you look at your friends and the qualities of each friendship, you will probably see areas in which there is something missing in the friendship. You may find that you can talk to one friend but not another; you may be able to laugh a lot with the second friend but not with the first. Perhaps you can talk and laugh with one friend about almost anything, but there is one subject you cannot bring up. There is a gap in the friendship.

Practice 43

A GAP IN MY FRIENDSHIP

Think of one of your friends and imagine the two of you together. Imagine a situation in which there is a gap in the friendship. How do you feel when this happens? Feel the sensations in your body. Relive your feelings at the time the problem occurs.

Now try imaginatively to get inside your friend's mind at the time of the problem. What is happening? Is your friend feeling tense and upset? Is your friend closing off feelings? Let yourself feel empathically your friend's re-sponses.

Lastly, try to put yourself into your friend's frame of mind in relation to this gap. Suspend all judgment, even if the judgment feels accurate. In your imagination let yourself be *your friend reacting to the problem. Sense the difference between judging from the outside and entering into the feeling of the problem empathically.*

Head a page of your journal "A Gap in My Friendship." Write about your experience with your friend. What is the gap? How does your friend feel about it? Could you sense the difference between judging and sensing from inside? Next, we will look at this difference between judging and not judging in compassion for a friend.

COMPASSION FOR A FRIEND: NOT JUDGING

> *Letting be is reverence; it is respect. It is what all true worship presumes, for it is letting God be God, letting self be self, letting suffering be suffering, letting joy be joy. With this letting be comes a growth into being and into identity with all these important energies of our lives.*
>
> MATTHEW FOX

> *Our great task is to prevent our fears from boxing our fellow human beings into characterizations and to see them as persons.*
>
> HENRI NOUWEN

There is an important difference between understanding and judging. Understanding is simply seeing the situation clearly and accurately from some framework. Judging is seeing the situation and evaluating it as right or wrong, good or bad, more or less valuable, from some framework.

Compassion often depends upon the suspension of judgment. This is very difficult sometimes. And in some situations you may decide that your values and commitments do not allow you to suspend judgment. Only you can make that decision. For the development of compassion, and an understanding of compassion as a way of being, you will need to practice not judging. You are *always* free to decide whether a situation requires judging.

Let me give you a personal example. I do not believe in killing. I have a general principle, a judgment, that killing is wrong.

In my moment to moment living I try to carry out that principle. I do not kill spiders that crawl around my house. I do not support war of any kind.

However, I *have* had the feeling of wanting to kill. Years ago, a man speeding drunkenly down our street came very close to running over my child and his friend who were playing near the curb. At that moment, if I had been holding a gun, I would have shot the driver of the car.

I can understand the fear, the need to survive, of a soldier in battle who shoots to kill. I can understand the desperation in a man who is being chased by the police and, running for his life, turns and kills.

I judge killing to be wrong. But I can feel compassion for those who have killed or who want to kill. When I feel compassion for someone who has killed, I am not judging. I am feeling the situation from the inside, feeling the suffering at that moment in that framework, and understanding the response.

Judging depends upon moral values and universal principles. All of us judge. Compassion also depends upon a moral value and a universal principle, but from a special framework: it is the value of being there with the other and feeling the other's suffering from within. The framework of compassion requires the suspension of judgment in the usual sense: the judging of another's actions from the outside as right or wrong.

In the next practices you will be asked to suspend judgment in the usual sense, and to feel compassion for a friend; to practice not judging. But our minds are very complex, very flexible, and capable of amazing connections. You can move back and forth between judging and not judging. You can hold in delicate balance your moral principles and your compassion.

You can remain open to the complexities of the situation and your own feelings. You can remain fluid and aware of what is happening at each moment.

Practice 44

NOT JUDGING

Think of a friend who has said or done something that you have judged to be wrong. It might be a friend on your list, but it also could be someone whom you did not list because you no longer consider that person a friend. Relive the whole situation in your mind. Relive whatever you were feeling when the event occurred.

Now, put yourself inside the mind of your friend. Relive the situation again, focusing on the other person's feelings. Is your friend upset? Is your friend absolutely certain about whatever he did? If your friend is certain, what is the source of that conviction? Try to sense the feelings behind that certainty. If your friend is uncertain, sense the confusion. Feel inside yourself whatever your friend is feeling. Is your friend suffering? In feeling this, can you now, at this moment, not judge?

Head a page of your journal "Not Judging." Write about the situation and your friend's thoughts or actions. Describe how you judged your friend. Then describe how you did not judge your friend. Let the two frameworks, judging and not judging, be there side by side.

If you want, talk to your friend about the situation. Let your friend know that you see the situation from his framework. Let your friend know about your own feelings, from your own point of view. If it makes sense in the context of your friendship, the two of you can do this practice together. You can work together on seeing situations from inside each other's perspective.

Practice 45

COMPASSION FOR A FRIEND WHO IS SUFFERING

Think of a friend who is suffering: choose a situation in which there is no judgment involved. You might have a friend who is sick or who has lost someone she loves. Imagine yourself together with this friend.

Imagine the two of you doing what you might normally do together. You do not necessarily have to be talking or referring to your friend's situation. Imagine a moment, now, when you sense your friend's suffering. Feel that inside you, as an actual sensation. Do you feel the connection between you? Do you feel that you want to be there for your friend?

Head a page of your journal "Compassion for a Friend Who is Suffering." Describe your friend's situation. Describe your own feelings. Did you feel the suffering as a sensation? In what sense did you feel that you wanted to help, or that you were in fact helping your friend?

Go to your friend. Stay empathically open. Let yourself feel whatever your friend is feeling. Be there, with your friend, in whatever happens between you.

Practice 46

HOW I FEEL WITH A FRIEND

This practice is concerned with your feelings in the presence of a friend. The next time you and a friend are together, and the external situation is relatively calm, take a few moments to focus on yourself. Does your body feel relaxed? Do you feel safe in this person's presence? Think of your touchstones for feeling upset and feeling peaceful. Is the feeling of being with your friend closer to being upset or being peaceful?

You can repeat this practice whenever you want. You will probably find that different friends accept and echo different kinds of feelings. You feel more alive with one friend, more peaceful with another. You already know this about your friends; put your knowledge into the framework of empathy, so that you can see your friendships with a different awareness.

LAUGHTER

> If my film makes one more person feel miserable I'll feel I've done my job.
>
> WOODY ALLEN

In discussing friendship, we spoke of laughter several times. Laughing with a friend is one of the strongest bonds of empathic connection. In the midst of a serious situation, one of you says something funny and you both step out of the usual way of seeing the situation. You see the thing from a different framework, a different reality. But what is so wonderful is that you are not alone; the two of you are there together in that different reality, on the same wavelength. And your feelings of release, insight, or connectedness happen together. Your laughter is like flying together to a special world.

Practice 47

LAUGHING WITH A FRIEND

For this practice, choose a friend who likes to laugh with you. Choose a friendship in which laughing together is an important part of the relationship.

The next time you are with this friend, stay particularly aware of your feelings. How do you feel when you first get together? How do you feel while you are laughing? How do you feel after you have laughed?

Head a page of your journal "Laughing with a Friend."

Describe your feelings. Did you feel, at any moment, perfectly tuned to each other?

If this feels right, talk to your friend about laughing together. Describe how you feel, and how it is important to you. Ask your friend how he feels when you laugh together. You know that being with this friend brings out certain feelings in you. Perhaps you feel more relaxed, more free, or more alive when you are with this person. Ask how you affect your friend. What feelings are being echoed between you in this friendship?

Practice 48

FEELING PEACEFUL WITH A FRIEND

There are certain friends with whom we feel peaceful. For this practice, choose one friend who brings a peaceful quality to your relationship.

The next time you are together, stay aware of this feeling. How do you feel when you first meet? How do you feel after being in each other's presence for a while? Can you sense yourself echoing your friend's peacefulness? Can you sense your friend echoing your own inner state?

Head a page of your journal "Feeling Peaceful with a Friend." Describe your feelings when you were together with this friend.

If you feel comfortable doing so, tell your friend about your sense of peace when the two of you are together. Ask how your friend feels. Does your presence give her the same feeling of peacefulness? Talking can give both of you insight into the empathic connection between you.

We laugh with one friend and feel peaceful with another. A third friend inspires us to do things we have always wanted to do. We know that our friends are important to us in unique ways. Each friendship is a different connection, and each connection echoes its own feelings.

Your friends can help enormously on your inner journey. You can go to one friend when you need laughter, and another friend when you need peace. You can explore feelings with a friend. The two of you together can discover empathy. You can let your friends help you, and you can discover much about yourself in being there for a friend.

In the next chapter we will discuss compassion for yourself. As you read that chapter, remember laughter. You can be compassionate toward yourself by letting yourself be playful, and by letting yourself *be*.

7 COMPASSION FOR YOURSELF

The only way to learn compassion is through your heart; you have to back up and pass through your own pain.

MATTHEW FOX

It is in my heart that I am whatever I am.   ST. AUGUSTINE

I understood the matters of wisdom and courage some time ago. I am just now beginning to understand the matter of compassion.

YAMAMOTO TSUNETOMO

To UNDERSTAND COMPASSION WE have to think about our vulnerability. Pain is a potential part of our world at every moment. This is our physical reality: our bodies are vulnerable and we will die.

The physical aspect of our vulnerability is pain; the mental aspect is suffering. Of course the mental and physical are intricately connected, but separating them for a moment helps in understanding the basic feeling of compassion. Suffering has many names: fear, agitation, anxiety, hurt, sadness, depression, despair. It is *emotional* pain.

People who have experienced extreme pain, and have confronted the reality of dying, have given us insight into the meaning of connection. They tell us that the nearness of death makes life more precious, and they speak of how beautiful each moment of living becomes, how happiness is felt in the smallest of gestures. They feel connected with everything that is alive.

The same kind of awareness comes to people who have struggled with suffering. People who have faced their own emotional vulnerability emerge with the recognition of everyone's vulnerability. They feel connected to everything capable of suffering. This sense of connection to everything vulnerable to pain and suffering is the basis of compassion.

This is why Matthew Fox says that we must pass through our own pain in order to reach compassion. When we open ourselves to the suffering of others, their suffering strikes a resonating memory of our own suffering. If we are afraid of our memories, we will be afraid of the suffering of others. We will close ourselves off to our feelings of compassion. As we face our own suffering, we can recognize and accept suffering in others.

Facing our own suffering, like facing our own death, is the difficult part of the path of compassion. There is another aspect of the path: the transcendence of suffering. Compassion for yourself means both facing your suffering *and* transcending it, even if only for brief moments of insight. Compassion for yourself means taking care of yourself, being there for yourself. It means knowing suffering *and* knowing freedom.

In the practices on empathy for yourself, you identified touchstones for feeling upset and feeling peaceful. In the next few practices, you will be able to identify more touchstones for feelings. These central experiences will help you to recognize each feeling calmly and clearly. Then, you can practice going from one feeling to another in taking care of yourself. You can move from fear to safety, for example, when you sense that you need to do this in compassion for yourself.

Practice 49

MY TOUCHSTONE FOR FEAR

Recall several times when you felt afraid. You might return first to a memory from childhood, and then think of a situation that happened just yesterday. Try to remember as much as you can about the actual sensation of fear, at a bodily and emotional level, each time. Pick one experience in which the feeling of fear was clear. Focus on that experience.

Head a page of your journal "My Touchstone for Fear."

Describe this central experience, giving the details of the situation and of the sensation of fear.

Think about the other times when you felt afraid. Were you alone in most of the situations or were you with another person? Is there any common element in the different situations? Add any insights you have about fear to your journal entry.

Practice 50

MY TOUCHSTONE FOR SAFETY

Recall several times when you felt completely safe. Again, it is often helpful to recall one memory from childhood and another from your recent life, but don't feel restricted to this combination. Relax, take several deep breaths, then breathe quietly. Let any memories, from whatever source, come to you. Then choose one experience that can represent the essence of safety for you. Let yourself relive that feeling.

Head a page of your journal "My Touchstone for Safety." Describe the experience and your actual bodily sensations. Were you alone or was someone with you?

Think about your other experiences of the feeling of safety. Is there a recurring structure in the different situations? It is best to let this unifying structure come to you as an insight, something that strikes you almost effortlessly. When something comes to you in this way, it is usually important to you. In your journal entry from above, write about this insight.

GOING FROM FEAR TO SAFETY: TAKING CARE OF MYSELF

> Knowing when to stop
> You can avoid any danger
> LAO TZU

Tuning into the presence of fear and safety can give you the freedom to move from one to the other. You are now more aware of the elements that constitute fear and safety for you. You are tuned to the presence of these feelings inside you. You also have looked at some of the situations in which you feel these emotions. You may have seen a pattern in these situations. This awareness can lead to inner freedom.

With this self-knowledge, you can choose more easily to avoid situations of fear. Compassion for yourself means recognizing that, for whatever reasons, you are frightened. It means accepting your feelings, and then caring for your self. How you care for your self will vary with the situation, of course. Sometimes, when you find yourself in a frightening situation, you can simply choose to leave. Sometimes, though, you cannot simply walk away from your suffering, just as when you are seriously ill you cannot walk away from the physical pain. But awareness can give you the strength to get through the suffering. As you take care of your body when you feel sick, you can also take care of your inner state. As you might hold a child who is afraid of the dark, you can calm yourself, knowing that fear is a human, acceptable emotion, and that the situation eventually will change.

As a more long-term goal, you can work toward being in fewer situations of fear and more situations of safety. You can decrease certain kinds of experiences and increase others. You can stop being with someone who frightens you, and be with someone who brings you a feeling of safety.

Practice 51

MY TOUCHSTONE FOR SADNESS

The word sadness *is used here to cover a group of feelings which include sorrow, depression, grief and despair. In developing your touchstone, use whichever word is closest to your experience. Recall that sense in yourself. Remember several situations when you felt that way. Then select one* experience that captures the essence of sadness for you. Re-live this touchstone of sadness.

Head a page of your journal "My Touchstone for Sadness." Describe your touchstone in detail, including the bodily sensations of the feeling.

Think back on the other experiences of sadness and see if there is a unifying structure. Do you have any insight about your sadness? Write about this insight in the journal entry for your touchstone.

Practice 52

MY TOUCHSTONE FOR ALIVENESS

Now, remember times when you felt especially alive. Again, the word itself is not important. You may think of this sense of aliveness as happiness, excitement, radiance, joy. Recall situations in which you felt this strong sense of being alive. Choose one experience as your touchstone for aliveness and relive this experience.

Head a page of your journal "My Touchstone for Aliveness." Write about your touchstone, including the bodily sensations and the situation you were in.

Return to the other situations of aliveness and see if there is a unifying structure. What is it like to feel really alive? What situations do you feel alive in? Add any insight you have to your journal entry above.

GOING FROM SADNESS TO ALIVENESS: TAKING CARE OF MYSELF

> But the slow large tears that spill from the eye, flowing like un-blown rain according to the laws of gravity and desolation— these are the real tears, I think. They are the ones that have been sim-mered, boiled, sieved, filtered past all anger and into the realm of serenity.
>
> M.F.K. FISHER

Sometimes we are not even aware of our own sadness. We are so busy worrying about other things that we are not tuned into ourselves. The first step in compassion for yourself is being tuned to your own inner state.

Sadness is often a part of healing after loss. The healing is helped by our awareness of the loss and its effect upon us. Awareness is a crucial element in lifting the sadness.

If the time is right, which is something only you can feel, you can choose to move from sadness to aliveness. You can decide to seek people and situations in which you feel lifted up, full of energy. Just the sense that you no longer need your sadness can make it lift. It is like facing your death, and afterwards feeling a connection to everything living. Facing your loss and the depth of your sadness can bring you to the other side, the sense of being connected to everything around you through the energy of life.

Practice 53

MY TOUCHSTONE FOR AGITATION

In terms of emotional rhythms, agitation is like aliveness gone out of control. Aliveness has a strong, steady, flowing beat; your whole body feels good and in tune with the surrounding world. The rhythm of agitation is uneven, strong and weak in unpredictable bursts, and physically uncomfortable. Your sense of agitation may be the same as your sense of being upset, which you examined earlier in the practices for empathy for yourself. Agitation includes a group of emotions: anger, rage, nervousness, anxiety. You can think of any one of these specific emotions that you experience. These emotions often include some form of physical pain: a tightening of the muscles, for example, that actually hurts. They are also, of course, a part of emotional suffering.

Recall several situations in which you felt agitated. Remember aspects of the situation: the place, the people, and any possible reason for your emotion. Try to relive the bodily sensations. Can you sense some part of your body becoming tense? Can you feel your muscles tightening? Is there any pain? Where is the pain located for you?

Choose one of these experiences as your touchstone for agitation. It can be the same experience as your touchstone for being upset. Choose an experience in which the feeling of agitation is clear and vivid.

Head a page of your journal "My Touchstone for Agitation." Write about the bodily sensations and the details of the experience.

Consider the several experiences of feeling agitated, and see if you find a recurring structure. Is there some part of your body which almost always experiences the pain? Is there some reason for your emotion that seems to occur in each of the experiences? Add any insights you have to your journal entry.

Practice 54

MY TOUCHSTONE FOR PEACEFULNESS

You identified a touchstone for peacefulness in the chapter on empathy for yourself. This sense of inner peace is so important, and sometimes so rare, that it is worth repeating, now, the practice of tuning into peacefulness. This time, focus on the rhythm of peacefulness for you. Focus on the sense of calm both within and around you.

Recall experiences in which you felt inner peace. Focus on the bodily sensations of that feeling. What seems to be happening inside your body? How does it feel? Focus now on the situations in which you felt peaceful. What are you doing in those situations? Choose one experience which represents the essence of peacefulness for you.

Head a page of your journal "My Touchstone for Peacefulness." Describe the experience, especially its rhythmic quality.

Think about the other times when you felt inner peace.
What were you doing? Were you alone? Were you with
someone? Were you in your own house, in the country, at
the ocean? Describe any insight that comes to you and add
it to your journal entry.

GOING FROM AGITATION TO
PEACEFULNESS: TAKING CARE OF MYSELF

Inner peace is the key: if you have inner peace, the external prob-
lems do not affect your deep sense of peace and tranquility.
THE DALAI LAMA

When we approach inner peace, the sense of being centered
and whole, we are approaching the transcendence of suffering.
If you have experienced even one moment of this peacefulness, you know it is real and that it can happen again.

You are probably aware of what things can upset you. You
can take yourself out of these situations whenever possible.

But once you have an awareness of inner peace, you are on
your way. You can slowly, steadily, increase the moments of
peacefulness, until they begin to replace the moments of agitation, and suddenly you find yourself centered and serene in the
midst of one of those awful situations. It is an amazing feeling.

COMPASSION FOR YOURSELF:
NOT JUDGING

Just when I found out the meaning of life, they changed it.
GEORGE CARLIN

We have talked about being aware of our own feelings and
of caring for ourselves. Caring for ourselves sometimes means
simply accepting our own feelings, allowing ourselves to be
there in the emotion. It also can mean sensing that it is time to
act, with a conscious decision to move from one way of being
to another.

But whatever form self-compassion takes, it also means not judging. Not judging is an aspect of all compassion.

We spoke about not judging as part of compassion for a friend. It is easy to see that we judge our friends. We reject certain people as possible friends because they lack some quality, and we get upset with our actual friends when they do things we think are wrong.

It is harder to see that we also judge ourselves. Sometimes, after a conversation, we feel upset. We feel that we said the wrong thing, but this judgment is not quite conscious. We are aware of a vague sense of not feeling at peace with ourselves. The judgment hovers around us. Sometimes it feels like a fog surrounding us. Without knowing what happened, we are lost. Awareness lifts the fog.

When we make a judgment, we are usually comparing some behavior of ours with a standard that we hold. Much of the time, the standard represents perfection, and the actual behavior cannot match the ideal. If we are aware of our ideal, and aware of our judgment, we can accept our behavior.

A pitcher in the major leagues judges his motion with every pitch. A dancer judges her balance and the flow of her movement at each moment of the dance. The athlete and dancer monitor their performances. This kind of judgment is done with awareness. Most of the time, people who work with concentration and commitment in a discipline are working toward an ideal: the perfect game or the perfect movement. They accept the fact that they make mistakes and they have off days. They know how rarely their ideal is actually experienced. They are patient with themselves. Awareness of your situation brings patience and acceptance, rather than blame.

Practice 55

JUDGING MYSELF

Think of a situation in which you suspect you are judging yourself without awareness. The best evidence of hidden judgment is that after the experience you do not feel at peace with yourself. You may feel upset, angry, or lost. Think of your touchstone for agitation. Your feeling after judging yourself may be close to that touchstone.

Head a page of your journal "Judging Myself." Describe what you do, how you feel, and your judgment. Is there some standard to which you are comparing your behavior? You may have trouble answering this question. If you can describe your ideal, and your feelings about that ideal, you will probably see how you are judging yourself. Your behavior does not fit with your ideal about how people should act or how things should be. Write down your standard as clearly as you can. Given this standard, what is your judgment about yourself?

Practice 56

NOT JUDGING MYSELF

Re-think the same situation, focusing empathically on your own feelings inside the experience. Let yourself feel your own emotions.

Head a page of your journal "Not Judging Myself." Describe the situation from inside your feelings. Now, across the bottom of the page, write down the standard against which you are judging yourself. Read your description of the situation and the standard together. Can you accept the standard as part of your thinking and still accept your own feelings in not judging your behavior? Can you hold the different parts in balance and accept them as parts of yourself? If, after seeing it written out clearly, you still feel that the standard is right for you, there is no need to give it up. You just accept both the standard and your behavior as parts of your life. You accept the past and the future as parts of the present moment. You accept yourself with compassion.

In the next chapter we will look at one of our most important relationships: our connection to our mothers. Keep alive your sense of compassion for yourself. Tuning into yourself and not judging will help you to be yourself with your mother and to accept her.

8 COMPASSION AND EMPATHY FOR YOUR MOTHER

A living love hurts. Jesus, to prove his love for us, died on the Cross. The mother, to give birth to her child, has to suffer. If you really love another properly, there must be sacrifice.

MOTHER TERESA

A mother who is in this state [of heightened sensitivity] can feel herself into her infant's place.

DONALD WINNICOTT

*I*N ONE SENSE, the empathic connection to your mother should be the easiest of all. When you were an infant, a natural empathic connection existed between you. You responded to the rhythms of your mother's body. Her steady heartbeat quieted you. In a completely nonverbal and unconscious way, this steady beat represented safety and peace to you.

You also tuned into other rhythmic patterns: the flow of her motions as she walked or moved her hands, the sound of her voice. You echoed her rhythms. This was the beginning of empathic communication. You learned the rhythms of emotion from this first connection.

You may still feel moments of this incredible connection. It seems that no matter what happens, how far away you move psychologically or physically, this bond remains. You can get a phone call from your mother and know almost before she starts talking if she is upset or peaceful.

But many of us have lost this connection. There are many possible reasons for this loss. Sometimes our mothers become so controlling that, as we grow up, we need to break the connection in order to become ourselves. Sometimes, our mothers themselves break the connection.

In this chapter we will look at ways of returning to the sense of connection with your mother. You can return in your mind, in your memories and your imagination. If your mother is living, and if you want to, you can go to her.

When a connection as powerful as this is broken, there is a lot of pain. Rather than being the easiest relationship, you may find this to be the hardest. Return to the practices of empathy and compassion for yourself as you go through this chapter. Remember that being connected to yourself is part of every empathic connection to another, so it will be part of reestablishing the bond between your mother and yourself.

Practice 57

EARLY MEMORIES OF MY MOTHER

For this practice, think back to childhood memories of your mother. Relax, take a deep breath, and breathe quietly. Let your mind wander to a moment when you were a child. Can you see your mother, feel her touch, smell her, or just sense her presence? Images can come in any of these sensory modes. Let several images of your mother come to your mind. It may take some time. You might remember an unusual moment, something with a lot of emotion involved, and you might also remember a quiet, ordinary moment—your mother sitting in her favorite chair or standing by the window.

Head a page of your journal "Early Memories of My Mother." Describe each image of your mother. What kinds of feelings do you sense from your mother in each case? Is she peaceful or agitated? Do you have a sense of her feeling safe or feeling fearful, feeling alive or feeling sad? Practice sensing your mother's feelings when you were a child.

YOUR MOTHER'S DREAM

It is sometimes hard to think of your parents when they were young. But of course they were hopeful and full of life, with dreams of their own future. Imagine your mother as a teenage girl, daydreaming about her life. What was your mother's dream?

We each have some image of what we would really like to do with our lives. Sometimes it happens. In many cases it doesn't, but it remains a vision, and often we are able to do other things that are related to the vision. Your mother may have spoken about her dream. You may have watched her doing things that enabled you to guess what it was. At certain moments, you may have empathically sensed her longing.

Practice 58

MY MOTHER'S DREAM

Think about your mother's dream. Put yourself back in your mother's place when she was a teenager and imagine her dream. Let yourself feel whatever she is feeling. Now, think about her life as you were growing up. Imagine her thinking about her vision. Feel whatever she is feeling.

Head a page of your journal "My Mother's Dream." Describe her dream. Describe her feelings as she thinks about it. Was she able to do things related to her vision? Did her vision in any way affect you? Write in your journal about anything that comes to you as you think about her dream.

YOUR MOTHER'S FEELINGS ABOUT HER ROLE IN THE FAMILY

Women in the past have been led to believe that they had no special contribution to make.

JEAN BAKER MILLER

Your mother's feelings about her role were probably extremely complex. Many women, when asked to name the most wonderful day of their lives, give the days their children were born. And when asked to name their most important accomplishment, they say the raising of their children.

There is incredible joy in the mother-child connection. We all yearn for the beautiful connectedness of empathy and compassion, being connected to another in a way that brings feelings of safety and trust and inner peace. And many mothers find this miraculous connection with their children. For some, this is the first time that they have known this feeling consciously, with adult awareness. Later in life they may seek and find the connection in other ways. But the birth of a child changes their lives profoundly, because then they see the possibility of a different way of life, the way of real connection.

But there are other aspects of a mother's role. There are situations of suffering related to the body's vulnerability, to the dangers in pregnancy, and to the sickness and death of a child. I want, however, to focus on situations which are not physical in this sense, but are created by society and the family structure. These situations are so upsetting, in part, because they are preventable. We cannot prevent the illness of a child and the great fear it brings us. But we can prevent the abuse of a child, the abuse of mothers, fathers and all living things. We can prevent the things that happen to mothers because of cultural ideas.

In thinking about your mother's role, some way that she suffered may strike you immediately. Stay with this insight and let yourself explore her situation from the framework of this insight.

It is also possible that in thinking about her role, you will see that your mother did not suffer in any significant way. If you know this, stay with this knowledge.

But if you are doubtful, as most of us are, there are certain questions you can ask yourself. Was your mother's work exclusively inside your home? If it was, did she seem powerless and less important to herself or to other members of the family? Because she wasn't making money and out there struggling in the *real world,* did she sometimes feel like a failure?

If your mother worked for a salary, if she was considered successful because of this, she still may have felt like a failure. This happens because she is carrying the weight of two jobs, inside and outside of the family, and cannot give her energy to both jobs fully and happily. Was she often exhausted? Did she feel guilty at times?

Finally, if your mother was a single parent, you probably felt the weight of responsibility she carried, and sometimes the loneliness. All of these ways that our mothers suffered are created by the pressures of her role. If being a mother and running a household had the same respect and understanding as being a doctor and running a clinic, our mothers would not feel like failures.

Practice 59

MY MOTHER'S FEELINGS ABOUT HER ROLE

Close your eyes, take a deep breath, and let your body relax. Take several deep breaths and let the tension flow out of your body with the breath. Breathe quietly when you are feeling relaxed. With your eyes closed, think about your mother when you were a child.

You might visualize her, sense her presence, or just let thoughts about her drift through your mind. Let whatever occurs to you happen. As you are thinking about her, put yourself in her role in the family. Place yourself, now, in her position.

Imagine her feelings about this role. If you can, relive those feelings. The feelings can be mixed and complex. Focus for a time on one feeling and then another. Let yourself feel, inside you, what you sense she felt then.

Head a page of your journal "My Mother's Feelings

*About Her Role." Describe whatever images and thoughts
came to you. What was her role? How did she feel about it,
at different times and with different people? Can you sense,
empathically, her feelings?*

YOUR SUFFERING AS A CHILD

*I do not agree with the big way of doing things. To us what mat-
ters is an individual.*

MOTHER TERESA

*Perhaps one can say that we are only alive when we live the life
of the world, and so live the sufferings and joys of the world.*

THICH NHAT HANH

As a child you were connected to your mother in intricate,
interdependent ways, and when she suffered you were bound
to sense it. This is a particularly clear example of the general
principle of compassion, that as living beings we are all connected, and any suffering can become *our* suffering.

With our mothers the interdependence is so strong, beginning with the physical interaction in the womb, that we rarely
even question it. We are not conscious of it; it is a given in our
universe. The empathic bond teaches us as infants that it is human and acceptable to laugh and be excited, and to cry and be
sad. As we get older, we learn more complicated forms of emotion from our mothers, more varieties of contentment and
suffering.

We suffer because of our connection to our mother. Some of
us were actually abused by our mother. This is the extreme of
suffering because of the closeness of the connection between
us. Some of us were abused, not directly by our mother, but
indirectly because she did not protect us. The rest of us, who
were not abused, were nevertheless hurt in certain ways by
our mother's problems. She may have been fearful, so that our

childhood was permeated with a sense that something was wrong. She may have been sad and withdrawn, so that we felt the pain of her pulling back from the bond between us.

Practice 60

MY SUFFERING AS A CHILD

For this practice, I want you first to return to the practices on compassion for yourself. Re-read your journal entries, and do over again whichever practices were most meaningful to you. Center yourself through your journal.

Then, recall a time when you were hurt by your mother. Relive the feelings you had as a child. This is not easy. But the suffering connected to your mother is part of your experience of compassion. It is the hope, and then the failure, of compassion.

Head a page of your journal "My Suffering as a Child." Describe how your mother hurt you. Describe your feelings. Let yourself feel whatever happens as you relive the situation.

YOUR GRANDMOTHER

Sometimes you have a bond with your grandmother that is free of the tensions involved with your mother. Your grandmother has worked out many of the difficulties of her life by the time you are born. She has a wisdom and peacefulness that draws you to her. She can accept and echo your feelings.

I never met my mother's mother, who died before I was born. I was named for her, and various adults told me stories about her as I was growing up. I cannot say why, but I feel I have become, in many respects, just like her. It could be genetic, and it could be that she provided a model for me that some instinct told me to follow. She was quite different from any other person in the family, and this difference allowed me to resist certain pressures to conform; it helped me to become myself.

When, as a child, you sense something about yourself, you look for someone who can echo and confirm that feeling. You search naturally for mutually empathic relationships. And if there is no one immediately around, you search for that bond anyway. Sometimes you are lucky enough to find a grandmother and, whether or not she is physically present, she is there in your mind, empathically present.

Practice 61

MY GRANDMOTHER

Think of your grandmother, your mother's or father's mother—whomever you felt closest to as a child. Recall several times when you were together with her, or when you were told stories about her. What feelings come back to you when you think about her? What was it like to be with her? Was there an empathic bond between you? Were there parts of you that were accepted and confirmed especially by her?

Head a page of your journal "My Grandmother." Describe the situations you remembered and the nature of the connection between your grandmother and yourself. Did you sense a connection to her that was unique in some way? Did you sense something like wisdom, patience, or inner peace? Did she give you a sense of freedom, or of being beyond the tensions you sensed in the usual adult world? What parts of you was she especially able to accept and confirm?

Thinking back now, do you think she provided a role model for you in any way? Did her presence as your grandmother help you in thinking about the different possible ways of living in your adult life? Write about your relation to your grandmother in your journal. If you want, you can repeat this practice later with your other grandmother in mind.

If your grandmother is living, and if you want to, go to her and tell her how she was important in your life. Talk about your memories of being together, empathically connected.

YOUR MOTHER'S AGING

> *. . . I used to live inside my mother. I lived there, inside her body for nine months. Can you imagine if somehow you were suddenly transported inside of somebody and lived there for nine months right now?*
>
> PETER LEVITT

Your mother is growing older. Her body is changing, and sometimes this change means a weakening of parts of the body; sometimes it means pain.

Most of us try not think about aging. We know that eventually it will happen to us, and it is easier not to think about it. But by avoiding it because of our own anxieties, we deprive our mother of empathic understanding. And we deprive ourselves of the freedom that comes from facing our anxiety and feeling at home with growing old.

Many older people say that they feel like a young person trapped in a body that is falling apart. Their minds have not changed. Their feelings are the same. They know how to ski down a slope and run through the woods in the rain. The pattern of movements, every muscle and nerve in each part of the body used in running and skiing, is stored in their mind. Their body, however, is unable to execute the movements.

Your mother may be afraid of aging. It is very frightening when parts of her body stop working, or work only with pain. Or, she may accept her aging peacefully. Whatever her feelings, you can be there for her empathically.

Practice 62

IMAGINING AGING

In this practice, I would like you to imagine your own aging. Close your eyes, and imagine yourself when you are very old. You are not sick or in pain. You are just aging naturally.

Imagine walking across the room. Each step is very small. You are aware of your balance with each shift in your weight. It takes you a long time to get from one end of the room to the other.

Imagine walking upstairs or down to the basement. Have you ever broken a bone in your leg, or injured an ankle? Recall the bodily sensations of walking up and down stairs. See yourself, at eighty, negotiating the stairs. Feel yourself concentrating on every motion so that you will not lose your balance. Feel the real danger of falling. Sense how slowly you move.

Head a page of your journal "Imagining My Aging." Describe your images of yourself. Could you sense yourself at eighty or ninety? Could you imagine being absorbed in each small movement?

Practice 63

MY MOTHER'S AGING

Imagine yourself, now, in your mother's place. In what ways is she aging? Does she move slowly? Is her balance precarious? Does she have any pain?

Let yourself feel whatever she feels as she moves around. If she is in pain, focus on that part of her body, and imagine the way it feels to walk, lift a box, or bend down. Put yourself inside her body and mind.

Head a page of your journal "My Mother's Aging."

Write about your experience of your mother's aging. How do you feel, now, about her aging? Did you sense fear, or acceptance, or some other emotion? You may have felt your mother's strength and courage. You may have felt her inner peace as her life slows down. Aging does not always mean suffering. But if she does suffer, let yourself feel it. Let yourself feel whatever she is feeling.

YOUR MOTHER'S DEATH

> *She straightened up a bit and said, "Don't hold me so tight, son, I am trying to move on."*
>
> R. PARAM BAINBRIDGE

> *. . . Know that the essence*
> *Will neither go nor stay.*
> SENG-TS'AN, THIRD ZEN PATRIARCH

If your mother is dead, you may want to think about her dying in the context of compassion and empathy. You can see her death in the framework of letting be.

Think back to your mother's death. If you were young, you probably did not understand what was happening. You may have felt a fog of confusion. Adults often make things worse for children by attempting to hide the truth.

If you were young, your mother left you at a time when you most needed her. You felt abandoned, lost or angry, or both. After her death, your life became difficult in many ways. You probably blamed her for leaving you to face these difficulties alone.

Elisabeth Kubler-Ross describes one of the stages of dying as letting go. A dying person begins to let go of attachments to the world. If you are tuned to the person, you sense that letting go. Your empathic response can help them let go. You can be there with them, echoing their feelings. You can help them feel the peacefulness of letting go.

If you were unable to be with your mother, whatever the reason, in this feeling of peacefulness, you can experience it now, in your mind. Her essence "neither goes nor stays."

Practice 64

My Mother's Death

Think about your mother's death. It may have been a long, painful illness. It may have been very sudden and unexpected. Recall the experience.

Imagine yourself with her now. Let yourself be with her in any way that comes to you. Imagine letting her go. Imagine feeling empathically that she is ready to leave, and echo that feeling. Let her be peaceful in leaving you.

Head a page of your journal "My Mother's Death." Describe whatever happened between you. You may want to do this practice again, letting different things happen each time.

YOUR MOTHER'S COMPASSION

> *There should be less talk; a preaching point is not a meeting point. What do you do then? Take a broom and clean someone's house. That says enough.*
>
> MOTHER TERESA

Mothers are known for their compassion. It is part of the image of a mother, and one of the things that makes the role so difficult. The way of compassion is only possible when compassion occurs freely. When it is demanded of us by outside pressures, it becomes an act, and we can suffer tremendously from the deception.

But usually our mothers' compassion is real and freely given. Then what is the problem? Why can this bond be so difficult? Because compassion cannot always be one-way. Compassion is not just sensing another's suffering, but wanting to do something. In the case of our mothers, compassion often takes the form of actually helping.

The problem occurs when a mother is the only one who is acting compassionately. It occurs when she has responsibility for all acts of compassion. No one can carry this kind of weight without a toll. There must be another being, who is there for her. When this mutual compassion is missing, her suffering can become unbearable.

Practice 65

MY MOTHER'S COMPASSION

In this practice, think about your mother's compassion. Let memories of her connection to you and others in the family drift through your mind. Focus on any memory that seems to give you some insight into your mother's feelings.

Head a page of your journal "My Mother's Compassion." Write about anything that came to you when you thought about your mother in the context of compassion. Describe your feelings about her compassion.

COMPASSION FOR YOUR MOTHER

> *Having seen the reality of interdependence and entered deeply into its reality, nothing can oppress you.*
> THICH NHAT HANH

Most of us want to return to the connection with our mothers. But we are not returning as children. We are returning with all of the complex parts of ourselves, including our present awareness. When we return, we are not the same.

If you return to the connection with your mother, it will not be the same connection. You will return to a bond that is based upon each of you being yourself, with all the intervening years of growth and wisdom. It will be a different bond.

If your mother is not living, you can create this connection in your mind, through memories and imagination. If she is living, you can first practice the connection in your mind, and then, if you sense it is right for you and for her, you can go to her.

Practice 66

COMPASSION FOR MY MOTHER

Imagine yourself together with your mother. Picture her in a familiar setting, a place where both of you feel at home. Think about the setting and the situation of her life, the details of the moment. Imagine her being empathically open to you. You may not be able to imagine her being open to all your feelings; find one feeling she can sense and echo.

Now imagine that both of you are open to one aspect of the suffering that has occurred between you. Let this aspect be the suffering of losing the bond between you. Imagine that both of you are feeling the sadness of this loss. Each of you wants to help the other transcend the suffering. You are feeling compassion for each other.

Head a page of your journal "Compassion for My Mother." Describe the scene you imagined. Describe the details: images, feelings, any words that were spoken, any actions. Did you feel compassion for your mother? Was the compassion mutual between you? Were you able to heal the suffering at least a little?

If your mother is living, and if you feel that you want to, go to her and talk about the connection between you. Tell her what you are feeling. You might want to show her this chapter as a way of beginning the conversation. Listen to her if she speaks of her own sense of the loss. If she is sick, or unable to talk, you can feel the closeness between you without words. Actually, you can feel it more clearly without words. But you may want to talk, once or many times, as a way of opening to each other's feelings.

There is, of course, another relationship which is just as important and just as difficult as the connection to our mothers. In the next chapter we will look at this relationship: our connection to our fathers.

9   COMPASSION AND EMPATHY FOR YOUR FATHER

*For me, helping Dad feel safe in his frailty and death, as he had
made me feel safe in my vulnerable infancy, was a completion.*

RAM DASS

*Spacious father who made me stand on my own,
Do not lose sight of me, protect me,
Fill me with a fatherly spirit,
For this long journey,
For this long journey.*

KOTARO TAKAMURA

YOU ARE GOING TO experience now, first with empathy and
then with compassion, your relationship with your father. If
you and your father are close to each other, the practices in this
chapter will deepen your awareness of your connection. If
your father is older, and depending upon you more and more,
your awareness can be, in Ram Dass's words, a completion for
you. You can be unified in facing your vulnerability together.

But if you and your father have not been close, this chapter
may be difficult for you. The relationship with your father may
be filled with memories of pain.

If your father is dead, you cannot go back and question him,
hold him, or ask him to hold you. You want to know why he
did certain things, why he caused you and himself pain. You
want to be able to forgive him, to forgive yourself, for failing
each other. It is hard, even impossible, to accept his dying. You
feel that it is too late.

But in one sense it is even harder if your father is still alive
and your relationship is not a good one. Then you have the recurring conflict of wanting to be with him and being unable
to do this, even though he is physically there, at most an

airplane ride away. You want to smash the wall that stands between you.

The following practices may give you a way of thinking and feeling that will help you with the wall. The idea is to practice this way of being with your father in your mind. It does not matter, for these practices, if he is living or not. He lives in your memory; he lives in the genes of every cell in your body; he lives in the connection between you, now and at every moment, the connection of feeling.

Practice 67

EARLY MEMORIES OF MY FATHER

Let your mind wander to images of your father from your childhood. Let these images of him drift through your mind. You might see him relaxing in his favorite part of the house, or working on something. A memory of some emotionally powerful event might come to mind. Focus for a while on these memories.

Head a page of your journal "Early Memories of My Father." Describe your father when you were a child. In each image, what did he seem to be feeling? Was he relaxed in one image and upset in another? Or did he seem to be the same in each image? Did he seem to be feeling safe or fearful? Was he open or closed to his own feelings? Describe your memories of your father's feelings when you were a child.

HOW YOUR FATHER MUST HAVE FELT WHEN YOU WERE A CHILD

> *I told him that my father was weak, and so was his world of ideal acts that he never performed. I was almost shouting. . . . 'You think you were stronger, don't you?' he asked in a casual tone.*
>
> CARLOS CASTANEDA

I am facing for the first time the serious realization that I cannot do all I dream of doing.

ELIOT DALEY

When you were a young child, your father was perhaps twenty or thirty years old. He had hopes, plans, and dreams for his life, just as you do. He may have wanted to sail around the world, be a judge, build his own house. He may have wanted an intimate, loving relationship with a woman. He may have wanted a steady job.

The events of his life unfolded; he was able to do some things and not others. What matters is that he felt longing and hope, fear and despair, just as you do. And you can tune into his feelings when he was a young father. By recalling certain memories you have of him, and tuning into his feelings at that time, you can begin to understand him from the inside. You can feel what he was feeling. Through these shared feelings, you are connected to each other.

Practice 68

MY FATHER'S DREAM

In this practice, recall a dream of your father's when you were a child. He may never have talked to you about it. As a child, you picked up information in a special way. You practiced, quite naturally, Freud's evenly hovering attention, letting everything flow into your mind. You picked up bits of conversation, facial expressions, and the energy of feelings. You sensed a certain energy in grown-ups when they were involved in something important to them. Try to remember something that you sensed was important to your father.

Close your eyes and imagine your father. Visualize him thinking about his dream. Imagine his feelings. Feel whatever it is that he is feeling. Sense the hope, the energy, he had as a young man. Feel the disappointment, the hope being crushed, if he felt that he failed. Let your father's feelings flow through you. Feel his dream with him.

Head a page of your journal "My Father's Dream." Write down his feelings as they came to you in the image, and your own response to his feelings. What are you feeling toward your father right now? Describe how you are feeling about your father after the practice.

THE HEAD OF THE FAMILY

> *You were such a giant in every respect. What could you care for our pity or even our help?*
>
> FRANZ KAFKA

> *My father's face was sad and lonely.*
> KOTORO TAKAMURA

Your father grew up in a world in which the man was the head of the family. Being *the head* meant being on top, the dominant one, the one in charge. It meant certain privileges; perhaps he went into that large world outside of the family and met important people, made important decisions, did important things. You were always waiting for him to come home.

As a young child you may have worshipped him. But as you grew older you probably began to sense his weaknesses, the gaps in that image of the perfect father: the man who could do anything and would always be there to protect you. Think how difficult it was for him to uphold this image. He was supposed to keep everything together. If there were problems over money, he was responsible. He was the person who had to fix things, to make everything work.

He was a human being, with fears and dreams for the future. He was given a role by society, and taught to hide his feelings. Feelings in our society are considered signs of weakness, of not being in control. Our heads must be cool and calculating, rationally making all those important decisions. The head in this view is split off from the rest of the body; it must control the body, which includes controlling the *weak* emotions. When the body represents the family, the father as its head is split off from his wife and children. They are allowed to show doubt and fear, but the father must keep these emotions hidden. Soon he learns to hide all of his emotions. He becomes his role. Imagine the isolation and loneliness of his position.

Practice 69

MY FATHER AS HEAD OF THE FAMILY

Close your eyes and imagine your father in some place where, as a child, you saw him often. He might be sitting at the head of the table or in his favorite armchair. Let yourself linger for a few moments on the image of your father: his face, his chest, his voice, his smell. Go back there with him when you were a child.

Let yourself feel, empathically, his loneliness. Sense how he would have liked to show doubt or hurt, but had to hold it all inside himself. Sense his separation from the rest of the family. Feel the loneliness coming from him and echoing inside you.

Head a page of your journal "My Father as Head of the Family." Describe your father. Describe his loneliness and your feeling of that loneliness. Did the empathic connection between you help to heal the loneliness? It is never too late to heal emotional pain. You and your father are connected to each other, always. Even if he is dead now, even if he is very old and doesn't remember, you are connected through your memories. You can talk to him and feel close to him through your mind.

YOUR SUFFERING AS A CHILD

I never could dance around you, my father. No one ever danced around you.

ANAÏS NIN

Your father suffered because of his role, but you suffered also, probably even more than he, because you were only a child. Perhaps, in his role as head of the family, he felt that he could not hold you and rock you. He had to be strong, to hide his emotions, and in the process he hid from you his compassion and love.

Even worse, he may have been the kind of father who hid all of his *weak* emotions but gave free rein to what society considers an acceptable emotion for a man—anger. So whenever he was feeling pain or fear or anything at all, it came out as anger, and you were the one who suffered from it. You were the one hurt with the awful power of his anger.

Virginia Satir describes each person in a family as connected to each other with an invisible rope. When the rope pulls one person, it pulls everyone. If your father suffered from his role, you suffered also. And as a child, that rope can be even more painful: you are so open, you have not learned how to resist, to turn off sensations. The rope which is there to comfort and protect you, instead snaps and brings you pain.

So, in this chapter, it is very important that while you relive these experiences, you feel compassion and empathy for yourself. Remember that you cannot feel connected to your father unless you feel connected to yourself. Compassion and empathy for your father are not sacrifices of yourself. They are bonds of feeling that can bring both of you a sense of peace.

Practice 70

My Suffering as a Child

Recall an experience in childhood when your father's behavior brought you suffering. Let yourself feel the emotions you had at the time, and your present, adult emotions. Try to stay open to all of your feelings. These are painful emotions, and as you relive the experience the emotions will exist as strongly as they did when you were a child. Practice feeling compassionate toward yourself.

*Head a page of your journal "My Suffering as a Child,"
and describe the experience. Write about the details of the
experience as much as possible; things like the furniture in
the room, the smell of the rug, the look on your father's
face. Describe all of your feelings. Is there any difference
between your feelings as a child and your feelings as an
adult reliving the experience? Do you feel compassion for
yourself?*

YOUR GRANDFATHER

You may have felt easier with your grandfather than with your
father when you were a child. The pressures that built a wall
around your father were decreasing for your grandfather. He
could look back over years of working and feel that he did
what he could. He had time to hold you on his lap. He may
have been changing quite deeply in his awareness. He may
have been facing his vulnerability as he aged. Facing the vulnerability of aging, he felt connected to your vulnerability as a
child.

For the next practice, choose one of your grandfathers,
whichever one you felt closest to as a child. You can repeat the
practice with your other grandfather if you want.

Practice 71

MY GRANDFATHER

*Think back on different images you have of your grand-
father when you were a child. Let these images drift
through your mind for a while. Then, focusing on each image, relive the feeling of connection between you and your
grandfather. What was the nature of the feeling between
you? Did you feel an empathic connection between you?
Did you sense that your grandfather accepted you in some
special way?*

Head a page of your journal "My Grandfather." Describe your connection with your grandfather. Was your relationship to your grandfather special in any way? Did he seem to have a sense of wisdom or inner peace? Were you empathically connected to each other?

Head a page of your journal "My Grandfather as a Role Model." Think about your grandfather's life, his way of thinking or feeling about things, as a possible model for you. Has he been, in any sense, a role model for you? Is something about him different from everyone else in your family? Is there part of you that is echoed by him more than any other person? Write about the importance of your relationship with your grandfather in your understanding of who you are.

If your grandfather is alive, you can go to him and let him know his importance to you in your life. You can tell him that you sensed his acceptance of you when you were a child, and what that meant to you. You can relive memories of being together.

YOUR FATHER'S AGING

> *But now, as Dad aged, I too was aging, and my passions were quieting enough that I could penetrate more deeply the rhythms of life.*
>
> RAM DASS

Seeing your father aging is seeing him become more human. It is seeing, starkly, his vulnerable nature.

How you approach his aging depends in part upon how he approaches it himself. The two of you are connected through feelings, as in every relationship, and his feelings about himself will affect you. You will echo each other's feelings.

Your father may be fighting his aging. If he has spent most of his life living up to the image of invulnerability, he will have a great deal of trouble accepting change. His body will not be as strong as he expects it to be. His mind will not be as incisive.

He will not be able to win his battles with the outside world. He will feel that he is no longer in control.

If your father looks at his world primarily from this framework, he will be afraid of aging. He may also be angry. In addition to fear and anger, he will feel confusion. He will not know who he is anymore. He is losing his invulnerable self, and he has not yet found his vulnerable one.

You cannot talk your father out of his fear and confusion. But you can be there for him empathically. If you receive and accept his feelings, you are accepting him as vulnerable and human. This will help him accept himself.

Aging can be seen from another framework. In aging, we can gradually free ourselves from all kinds of pressures and fears. You looked at this aspect of aging when you remembered your connection to your grandfather. As we grow older, we begin the process of leaving the ordinary world. This can mean many different things: not caring so much about what other people think of us; listening more to our own instincts; accepting feelings of weakness in others; accepting our own vulnerability; becoming empathically aware.

Ram Dass speaks of the rhythms of aging as the rhythms of life. The rhythms of aging are quiet and slow. In the practices, when you close your eyes and imagine a situation, time slows down: the past, your memories, become part of the present moment. The future, your plans, are also right there in the present moment. In your inner world, everything is contained in the moment of your reflection.

Time is very much like this for older people. It is often said that older people live in their memories. We can also say, however, that older people live in a different reality. They do not live only in the past; they are often acutely aware of the present moment. They sense your presence, and they pick up your feelings. They can be unaware, however, of activity in the ordinary world: they don't care about the date, or the latest political election. In the ordinary world, time marches on, and we often march with it. In aging, as their rhythms slow, older people can enter a world of calmness and inner peace.

Practice 72

THE SLOWING OF TIME

In this practice, imagine that you are very old, perhaps eighty or ninety. You are sitting in your favorite chair by the window. Breathe deeply and relax. Let your bodily rhythms slow down. Let your breath be slow and quiet.

Look around you at the world. Look at the people rushing by. Look at the cars speeding to their destinations.

Now focus on the people in your family. See them from your new framework. They are all doing things: getting ready for appointments, preparing things, fixing things. You are just sitting there, watching. How do you feel? Do you feel peaceful? How do you feel about the other people?

Head a page of your journal "The Slowing of Time." Write about your experience. Were you able to imagine yourself as eighty or ninety years old? Did you feel the slowing of time?

Practice 73

MY FATHER'S AGING

Close your eyes, and put yourself in your aging father's body and mind. If your father is having problems with some part of his body, focus on the problem. If he is in pain, feel the pain.

Think about your father's feelings. Is he afraid? Is he fighting his aging? Has he accepted his aging and found a sense of peace? For this practice, it is important to tune into your father's feelings, no matter what they are. Imagine yourself in your father's mind. What is he feeling about his aging?

Head a page of your journal "My Father's Aging." What did you sense empathically about your father? Were you able to accept your father's feelings? Write about your father's aging.

YOUR FATHER'S DEATH

If you were present when your father died, and you were both able to accept his leaving, you have had a powerful experience of connection. Many of us missed this experience. Our fathers died in some faraway place. They died suddenly, sometimes violently. In some cases we were children, not allowed into our father's room.

Saying goodbye to your father means accepting his leaving. It is being with him empathically. When you say goodbye, you are saying that it is all right to die. You are saying that you feel his need to leave. You feel with him the peacefulness that comes at the end.

In the following practice, you can say goodbye to your father.

Practice 74

MY FATHER'S DEATH

Imagine the situation of your father's death. How did he die? Who was with him?

Imagine being with him when he was dying. Feel whatever he is feeling. Be there for him empathically.

Try to let him go. If you can, say goodbye to him.

Head a page of your journal "My Father's Death." Describe your father's death. Then describe the scene that you imagined between you.

A BOND OF COMPASSION
WITH YOUR FATHER

> *What is of most moment in compassion is not feelings of pity but feelings of togetherness.*
>
> MATTHEW FOX

If you want to take something
you must first allow it to be given.
LAO TZU

You have experienced some of your father's pain. It is also your pain. As a child you suffered because of his problems.

And your father suffered because of his own father's problems. He suffered because of the role he was given as father and male.

All of us suffer, each in different roles at different times of our lives, but ultimately, whatever our roles and conditions, we suffer because we are human. This is our connection, our bond, and through this bond with each other we can transcend the suffering. If our lives were all suffering and pain, we would not know it; we would accept it as we accept the air we breathe. We know suffering because we know the moments of not suffering, the moments of feeling completely safe, of feeling happy. We reach these moments through connection with others. In our connections, by being really there with each other, suffering dissolves. There is no more loneliness, no more fear. The connection brings inner peace.

In the next two practices, you can work on creating a bond of compassion with your father.

Practice 75

MY FATHER'S COMPASSION

I want you to imagine a moment when your father felt compassion for you. It can be a very simple moment. It can be an image from childhood when he lifted you up and held you in his arms. It can be just a look, a glance he gave you across the dinner table, when you were older. Remember one moment, any moment, when you sensed that he felt your suffering as his own.

Close your eyes and recreate this moment. Relive your feelings. Feel the importance to you of this single act of your father's compassion.

Head a page of your journal "My Father's Compassion."
Describe the moment of his compassion. What were you
feeling? How important to you was his recognition, his un-
derstanding? Write down the meaning to you of your fa-
ther's act of compassion.

Practice 76

COMPASSION FOR MY FATHER

In this practice, I want you to imagine a scene that may
never have happened. If it did, you have experienced something very special. If it did not, you can experience it now
in your imagination. And perhaps it actually can happen.

Close your eyes and imagine your father in a familiar
setting. He is alone there; imagine the room, the furniture,
the smell of the room, the feel of things in the room. Add
details about your father that come to you; perhaps the
position of his body, the tilt of his head, his hair, his eyes,
the feel of his clothing, the texture of his skin, his smell.
Watch him for a while from the distance.

Now enter the room. Stand in the doorway and let him
see you. At this moment, he is the person who felt compassion for you, who responded to your suffering. Feel his suffering. Let the feeling radiate from inside you toward him,
so that he knows that you sense his pain. If you can, walk
toward him. Feel his suffering the way you would feel the
suffering of a frightened child. If you can, hold him and let
him hold you.

If your father is living, and if this is right for you, try to
create this scene together with him. You may want to begin by talking to him about his life. You can recall memories of the two of you together when you were a child.
These memories can be both happy and painful. If you
stay open, you cannot avoid the memories of suffering.
You may be able to face them together. You can work out
the details in your own way.

You may find that talking creates blocks to an openness to feelings; your father may return to the barriers set up by his old role. If your father is sick, talking may exhaust him. Listen to him, and talk only if it seems to be helping. Stay open to the feelings between you. Echo his feelings. Let him know, in whatever way makes sense in your relationship, that you are there with him in that moment.

In the next chapter we will look at a special situation, mutual empathy in an intimate relationship. We search all our lives for an empathic being, someone with whom we are perfectly tuned. For some of us, this mutual empathy is realized in an intimate relationship.

10 MUTUAL EMPATHY IN AN INTIMATE RELATIONSHIP

Intimacy is empathy.

JANET LEVY

Even remembering union, without the embrace, the transformation.

ZEN FLESH, ZEN BONES
SANSKRIT TEXT, TRANSCRIBED BY PAUL REPS

So each individual has awareness for the things they truly identify with. Identification is love.

LOUISE NEVELSON

*W*E HAVE EXPLORED COMPASSION and empathy in several relationships, and you have experienced moments of empathic connection. You have felt the intimacy of being inside the other person through feelings.

Do you remember laughing with a friend? Do you remember quieting a child and feeling the child's calmness calming you? You were there together, feeling the same thing at the same time.

Empathy that occurs for both of you at the same time is called *mutual empathy.* You are simultaneously tuned into each other. These are special moments in any relationship, moments of shared insight into the nature of the self and the connectedness of the world.

Mutual empathy occurs in all our relationships. But there is one kind of relationship in which its presence almost defines the relationship. This is an intimate relationship, a love relationship which usually includes sexual union. We want to be there for our children; we want our parents to be there for us;

but in an intimate relationship, we want to be there for each other. We search for that bond of self and other that makes us one.

In this chapter we will explore mutual empathy in an intimate relationship. The other person can be with you now, or can come from the past or the future. The details of the relationship are only important as they affect the empathic connection between you. In the practices, I will assume that you are with the other person now. If this is so, I hope that the two of you will work on deepening mutual empathy together.

Practice 77

Mutual Empathy: My Touchstone

Let your mind drift to moments of special closeness with the other person. Focus on one experience in which the empathy seemed to be mutual: you were there for each other, feeling the same thing at the same time. You were aware of the connection between you. Recall the experience and relive the feeling. This will be your touchstone for mutual empathy.

Head a page of your journal "Mutual Empathy: My Touchstone." Describe the details of the experience, the situation of the other person, your own situation, and your experience together. Describe each of your feelings. Did either of you do anything or say anything? Do you remember any special details? Describe as much as possible the feeling that the empathy was mutual.

Practice 78

Mutual Empathy in Silence

My heart in this moment splits, drops away
and in the sharp silence becomes one with the universe that
wraps us two.

Kotaro Takamura

Mutual empathy often happens in silence. Perhaps our minds are quieted by the absence of speech, allowing us awareness of other modes of communication.

Think of a time when you were sitting silently with the other person and you felt very connected, in tune with each other. The connection could have been based upon mutual peace or mutual anxiety, it doesn't matter. It could have been a sense of relief at being together after some difficulty or separation. You weren't talking. You were just there together. Think of two or three of these experiences if you can. For contrast, think of a time when the silence between you was awkward.

Head a page of your journal "Mutual Empathy in Silence." Describe the details of each experience of silent empathy.

Read the descriptions in your journal entry above. Do you see any common thread? Is there some unifying structure in the experiences of silent empathy? Let any insight come to you about these experiences of mutual empathy in your relationship, and add it to your journal entry.

MUTUAL EMPATHY IN A CRISIS

> *My heart leaps, dances, flaps about*
> *exactly as you move,*
> *but never forgets to protect you,*
> *my love.*
>
> KOTARO TAKAMURA

We usually pull together in a crisis. The danger and intensity of the experience shake us into a higher awareness of what is important to us. We are feeling the same things: fear, the need to be close, the desire to protect each other. This shared feeling, and the heightened awareness created by the importance of the crisis, enable mutual empathy to occur. The crisis takes us out of our ordinary, habitual world. We are transported to a new framework, a new sense of reality. Carlos Castaneda called this *stopping the world*.

But mutual empathy can be absent in a crisis, and because we are counting on each other, its absence is especially painful. In the next three practices we will look at mutual empathy during a crisis. The purpose is to gain some insight into how you can be there for each other when you both need protecting.

Practice 79

THE PRESENCE OF MUTUAL EMPATHY IN A CRISIS

Think of a time of crisis when mutual empathy was present between you. Recall the experience, the situation as it affected each of you, and the feeling of mutual empathy. Let yourself relive that feeling.

Head a page of your journal "The Presence of Mutual Empathy in a Crisis." Describe the crisis as it affected each of you. Write about the feeling of mutual empathy in the crisis.

Practice 80

THE ABSENCE OF MUTUAL EMPATHY IN A CRISIS

Think of a time of crisis when mutual empathy was not there between you. Recall the experience and the situation as it affected each of you. Relive the feeling of the absence of mutual empathy between you.

Head a page of your journal "The Absence of Mutual Empathy in a Crisis." What was the nature of the crisis? In what ways did it affect each of you differently? How did it feel when mutual empathy was not there between you?

Practice 81

COMING TOGETHER IN A CRISIS

Read your two journal entries, the presence and the absence of mutual empathy in a crisis. What enabled mutual empathy to occur? What might have prevented it? What was its effect on your relationship? What was the effect of its absence?

Head a page of your journal "Coming Together in a Crisis." Write about any insights you have in comparing the two experiences.

MUTUAL EMPATHY IN DIFFERENT LIFE EXPERIENCES

> *I never saw a moor,*
> *I never saw the sea;*
> *Yet know I how the heather looks,*
> *And what a wave must be.*
> EMILY DICKINSON

In an intimate relationship we seek a quality of union that we do not expect in other relationships. We seek an emotional connection, regardless of the external situation. We accept the reality of at least two worlds, one internal and one external. The external world can create chaos in our lives, separating us and even bringing death. But in an intimate relationship, we expect that throughout the physical separation, we will be emotionally together. Throughout the separate problems of our external lives, we will be there empathically.

When empathy is blocked in an intimate relationship, it is especially painful. When empathy is blocked, the essence of the relationship, the internal union, is gone too. Sometimes, the block begins with a difference between the two of you in the external world. There is some difference in your life experiences: only one of you has a child; only one of you has been very poor; only one of you has been successful in some special way. In other relationships you expect and accept these life differences. Large differences in experience are built into the structure of your relationships with your parents and your children. But in an intimate relationship these differences can threaten your internal connection. You may have difficulty putting yourself in the other person's place. Although you try to understand, you may find yourself misinterpreting things. You are not quite sensing what the other is feeling.

The broken connection that is troubling you is troubling the other person too. There is a feeling of confusion between you. You lose touch with each other in the fog of this confusion. You lose that echoing awareness.

But you have seen that empathic awareness can be developed. Together, you need to sift through your differing conceptions of the situation in order to reach the essential emotions—very basic emotions such as fear and safety. Each of you knows what it means to feel afraid and to feel safe.

Reaching these emotions together may not be easy. But the confusion can be patiently unraveled if the two of you work together. The problem is not so much in the difference, as in the emotions that go *with* the difference. You can feel threatened, left out, and abandoned by each other. These feelings are strong enough to block out all other feelings. You close the gate between you. If you practice together, the openness will return.

Practice 82

DIFFERENT LIFE EXPERIENCES: TUNING INTO THE OTHER PERSON

Think of a situation that the other person experienced, which you have never known: a serious illness, for example, or great insecurity in childhood. This difference in experience may have created hurt and confusion between you.

Ask the other person to tell you one basic emotion created by the experience. Focus on a basic emotion, such as fear or safety. Think of a situation in which you felt this same emotion. Remind yourself that although the situations were very different, the feeling was basically the same.

Complex situations create complex, or mixed, emotions. Ask the other person to help you identify a second emotion involved in the experience. Recall a situation in which you experienced this same emotion. If you can, think of a situation in which you felt this same combination of emotions.

Ask the other person if there is a third feeling involved. Talk to each other about the emotional meaning of the experience. Practice tuning into each separate feeling until you feel empathically tuned to the other person's feelings as a whole.

Head a page of your journal "Different Life Experiences: Tuning into the Other Person." Describe the experiences and the emotions involved. Were you able to tune into the other person's feelings to some extent? This practice is difficult and you may want to repeat it regularly. If you are working together, do the practice with the other person tuning into one of your experiences.

Practice 83

DIFFERENT LIFE EXPERIENCES: HELPING THE OTHER TUNE INTO ME

Think of an experience in your life that the other person has never known. Again, this difference may have created confusion between you.

Try to let the other person know what you are feeling. It will probably be complicated. Sift through the layers of the experience and get to one basic emotion. Are you afraid? Are you feeling a sense of freedom? Describe what you are feeling in the simplest way, without violating the truth of the feeling. Do this for a second or third feeling that is part of the experience for you.

Remain empathically open to the other person's feelings. He or she may be anxious about not understanding, or hurt at being left out of your experience. Do whatever you have done in the past to let the other person know you are still there. There are some experiences that you, at some level, must go through alone. But at the level of feelings you can be together.

Head a page of your journal "Different Life Experiences: Helping the Other Tune into Me." Describe your experience and how it differed from the other person's. Were you able to sift through the layers to get to your basic emotions? Did you sense that the other person became less anxious and more open as you uncovered your own feelings?

If you are working together, repeat this practice, changing your roles.

Talk together about what happened to each of you in the practices. Stay open and aware as you listen to the other person and to yourself. In trying to help the other person understand, each of you will be deepening your understanding of yourself as well. You will be developing mutual empathy together.

SEXUAL EMPATHY

> When in such embrace your senses are shaken as leaves, enter this shaking.
>
> ZEN FLESH, ZEN BONES
> SANSKRIT TEXT, TRANSCRIBED BY PAUL REPS

> Take me to you, imprison me, for I
> Except you enthrall me, never shall be free,
> Nor ever chaste, except you ravish me.
> JOHN DONNE

> By night on my bed I sought him whom my soul loveth.
> THE SONG OF SOLOMON

One of the most extraordinary forms of connection to another person is sexual union. The oneness that we search for at
an emotional level is there also at the bodily level; we are unified within ourselves in body and mind, and we are unified
with the other person.

The flow of mutual empathy is at the heart of sexual union.
Your bodies are moving in the same rhythm and your feelings
about each other and the experience are the same. You are aware
that the other is feeling the same thing you are feeling. The
awareness of sameness increases the intensity of your own feeling, which in turn increases the intensity of the other's feeling,
in a spiraling effect. You are focused together on the rhythm
of body and feeling. This is mutual empathy in a very pure form.

Many partners experience orgasm together, not because of
some special physical compatibility, but because of the synchronicity of emotional rhythms. We sometimes hear that we
shouldn't worry about simultaneous orgasms, and of course
we shouldn't *worry* about it. But the implication is that rhythmic synchronicity is unimportant. If we are thinking only of
the bodily level, perhaps this is true. But we know that our
bodily rhythms are connected to our emotional rhythms, and
we want to be rhythmically together through the whole experience. We want the connection to be as close as possible. We
yearn to come together as one.

RHYTHMIC STRUCTURE

> *The way one's body moves and feels in the presence of the other*
> *reflects exactly what is going on in the relationship.*
>   GAY HENDRICKS AND KATHLYN HENDRICKS

Time is part of the deepening of intimacy. Something brought
the two of you together, some sense of the possibility of connection. You felt some sense of safety in living your lives together. In this space of safety and connection, awareness of
each other deepens.

You begin to learn signs of each other's feelings. You see meanings in each other's movements: facial expressions, bodily positions, hand motions. You echo each other's rhythms: the breath, the speech, the heartbeat. You feel meanings in the fastness or slowness of certain rhythms, rhythms of eating, walking, touching, and making love.

In an intimate relationship the deepening of the empathic connection never ends. You don't one day say, "Ah, now I understand everything." As each of you grows in self-awareness and opens to more of your own feelings, you are able to open to those feelings in the other person. And as you become more open to the other person, echoing and accepting rhythms of emotion, you get in touch with these rhythms in yourself. Self-empathy and mutual empathy grow together. It takes time and the practice of awareness.

Practice 84

RHYTHMIC STRUCTURE

Think of a time when you empathically sensed the other person's feelings. Imagine the other person at this moment of your empathic awareness. Is there something about the motion or stillness of the body that strikes you as meaningful? Can you identify anything about the other person's bodily rhythm that seems connected to the feeling? Can you feel that sense of the bodily rhythm echoing inside you? Relive your awareness of the other person's body at that moment, and your awareness of your own body reflecting the connection.

Head a page of your journal "Rhythmic Structure." Write about your perceptions.

MUTUAL COMPASSION

Mutual compassion flows naturally from mutual empathy in an intimate relationship. When one of you suffers, both of you feel it. A crisis especially heightens your awareness of each other's vulnerability, and the vulnerability of your union. And this awareness leads to the desire to hold and protect each other in compassion.

We have looked at two aspects of compassion in different relationships: the compassion of helping, and the compassion of letting be. Both of these possibilities must be there in an intimate relationship. Empathic perception means sensing when the other person wants help, and sensing when they want to be left alone. Mutual compassion sometimes means protecting each other, and sometimes means giving each other freedom.

Practice 85

When I Really Help

Think of a situation in which you do something that helps the other person. Ask the other person about something you do that really helps.

How do you feel about the situation? Do you feel the other person's suffering? Do you want to help or do you resist? In the act of helping, what thoughts or feelings do you have? Can you sense that your action is really helping the other person? Do you sense that he or she feels differently after your help?

Head a page of your journal "When I Really Help." Describe the situation. Write about your feelings, and the feelings of the other person.

If the two of you are working together, repeat this practice, changing your roles. Tell the other person of something he or she does that helps you. After you have both done the practice, talk about the ways you are able to help each other. Are the situations similar or very different? Are your feelings about helping each other, and accepting help from each other, the same? Talk about the ways in which you help each other.

Practice 86

WHEN THE OTHER PERSON NEEDS ME

For this practice, think of a situation in your relationship in which you close off the other person's feelings of suffering. Ask the other person to tell you about a situation in which they feel a need for your presence, but you are not there. You close the gate.

Work on doing something for the other person when this situation occurs. It can be anything. Mother Teresa said, "Pick up a broom and clean . . ." The essence of this act of compassion lies partly in its comforting quality: a person feels better in a clean room. But the act of sweeping, in addition to being comforting, is unexpected. The person is expecting talk and preaching. Sweeping is like bringing sunlight and fresh air; it is giving something new; it is opening awareness. In your own relationship, do something for the other person that is different from your usual ways of acting. If you rarely talk, talk. If you always talk, be quiet.

If the two of you are working together, repeat this practice, reversing the roles.

Practice 87

WHEN I AM ABLE TO LET THE OTHER PERSON BE

Think of a situation in which you are able to let the other person be. Ask the other person for an example. Find a situation in which the other person wants to be left alone, and you do this. You are able to leave the room, or stay and remain quiet, as an act of respect and compassion.

Head a page of your journal "When I Am Able to Let the Other Person Be." Write about the situation and your feelings. Is it difficult for you to leave the other person alone? How do you feel about the person when you do this? How do you feel about yourself?

*Now you can tell the other person about a time when he
or she lets you be. This is a situation in which you want to
be quiet; you want to be alone. Repeat the practice. Then
talk about your experiences. Is letting be easier for one of
you? In letting each other be, do you feel a sense of trust?
Talk to each other about what you are feeling.*

Practice 88

WHEN I NEED TO LET THE OTHER PERSON BE

*For this practice, think of a situation in your relationship
in which you help or protect the other person habitually.
Talk to each other about this act of helping. Ask the other
person if he or she is ready to be left alone in this situation.*

*When you do something out of habit, you usually lose
awareness of the feelings involved in the act. Get back in
touch with these feelings. Does the other person still need
your help? Does he or she feel a need for the freedom to
work things out alone? Follow your empathic sense of the
feelings involved in this situation. Let yourself see the situation from a new framework, not from habit. Let the other
person be.*

*Letting be is sometimes the hardest thing to do in an in-
timate relationship. Repeat this practice with the other
person letting you be in some situation. Work together on
seeing situations with each other's feelings. Gather awareness through doing the unexpected, giving each other unexpected help or unexpected freedom.*

Practice 89

MUTUAL COMPASSION AND EMPATHY
IN MY RELATIONSHIP

*For this practice, read through all of your journal entries
for this chapter. Think about mutual compassion and*

empathy in your relationship. Let yourself stay open to your feelings, whatever they are.

Head a page of your journal "Mutual Compassion and Empathy in My Relationship." Write about your insights and feelings. Let your thoughts come as freely as possible.

We have looked at the close connection between intimacy and mutual empathy in a love relationship. If you think back to times when you and the other person felt the deepest intimacy, you will discover that mutual empathy was part of the experience. In sexual union, in facing a crisis together, or in just being there for each other, mutual empathy is at the center of the connection. In this intimate relationship the two of you can work together to increase awareness. This is a special, magical kind of work.

In the next chapter we will look at empathy and compassion in the presence of enemies and strangers. We will approach empathy as a perceptual ability which gives us information, sometimes essential survival information, about the world around us.

11 COMPASSION AND EMPATHY FOR ENEMIES AND STRANGERS

The soul selects her own society,
Then shuts the door.
EMILY DICKINSON

All humans, friends, enemies and strangers, those close and
those distant, have to experience birth, illness, pain and the fears
of loneliness, old age and death.
GESHE KELSANG GYATSO

COMPASSION AND EMPATHY CROSS traditional boundaries and bring an understanding that can change our lives. We are going to look at four situations of compassion and empathy that cross boundaries in unusual ways. We will look, first, at a person who faces, as her daily work, the pain and suffering of people who are almost strangers. The two situations that follow involve our responses to people we think of as enemies. The last situation deals with our empathic perception of danger in the presence of a stranger. These are intense examples of our connections to others which can bring us insight.

COMPASSION AS A WORKING COMMITMENT

Ultimately, you can always be there.
RACHEL COHEN

Wholeheartedness of attention means being there altogether in
the service of the patient, yet with a kind of self-forgetfulness.
KAREN HORNEY

Listening to the radio or watching television, we hear about the suffering of someone we do not personally know, even a fictional character, and we feel something in our chest. We feel connected in our vulnerability.

But there is an enormous gap between the feeling of compassion and the ability to work with those who are seriously suffering. People who have chosen this kind of work have made a special commitment to compassion.

Rachel Cohen is a nurse in a bone marrow transplant unit of a Boston hospital. Patients go there when they are facing their own deaths. It is a place of last resort.

The treatment requires that the patient be kept as sterile as possible. Everyone entering the room must wear a mask, gown and gloves. Imagine yourself going to visit the patient. You enter the room wearing isolation clothing. You and the patient are surrounded by enormous, blinking equipment. There can be no skin to skin contact between you. And the other person is very sick.

Most people in this situation are frightened. They sit far away from the patient, afraid to touch even through the gloves. For the patient, all normal contact is gone.

"When you go into that room, you are their link," says Rachel Cohen. "You are the one who is open to their pain. Compassion basically means being able to open up to whatever is going on. It means seeing something ugly and not allowing yourself to leave the room."

Leaving the room, Cohen explains, doesn't necessarily mean physically walking out. Leaving means not being there for the patient. It can take the form of looking down at the chart instead of into the patient's eyes. It can mean hiding behind the equipment and the role. "You draw the line; you shut the door; you're out of there."

"The most comfortable way of being with a patient," she goes on, "is when you are being compassionate. When you hide behind the equipment it feels like thickness. You know when you're closing off. And it is obvious to some patients that you are in the room but not really there."

There are times of compassion and times of not being there for all of us. What makes the greatest difference between these times, she explained, is how secure you feel about yourself in your role. When you are not clear about yourself, you hide behind the role.

"Usually," she says, "I close off because of something going on inside myself. To get back there, I just take a deep breath. And I say to myself, 'I'm not going to deal with *me* right now.'"

In speaking to Rachel Cohen and others who work professionally with those who are suffering, I noticed something very important. Each of these professionals, without exception, spoke of their struggle to stay open. Each described times when they became unaware, when they closed the door. They envisioned their job, most importantly, as staying *aware,* and they recalled the times of failure, not from guilt or lack of self-compassion, but as a reminder of how easy it is to slip away. These people work hard at consciously being there with the other person in the moment. Rachel said: "You can always be there."

THE ENEMY IN WAR

> *When we have inner peace, we can be at peace with those around us.*
>
> THE DALAI LAMA

In order to have a war there must be an enemy. This is true of any war, whether it is global, or between two cultures, or even a war against drugs. Relating to others within the framework of war means closing off our compassion for the enemy. It means seeing the other as an object which must be eliminated. It means not seeing the situation from the framework of that other person, not feeling the other's fear or pain. That other person, of course, is not feeling your pain. And so you both attack, and in war, that means you kill and die.

When our country was at war with Iraq, Iraq was the

enemy. But it was hard for us to hate the *people* of Iraq. We felt compassion for the children who were frightened and hungry. We even felt, empathically, the fear and desperation of the Iraqi soldiers. That is why Saddam Hussein became, in the culture of war, a devil, the personification of evil. By placing all of the blame on him, we were able as a culture to keep our compassionate feelings for the Iraqi people as a whole.

The Vietnam war deeply altered our understanding of ourselves as a nation. In trying to sort out the pain and the anger that we had toward the enemy and toward each other, we had to come through a difficult journey of recognition. As a nation we had to go back through our own pain. As awful as the war was, it made us more compassionate as a society. Veterans and war protestors alike have tried to see and feel the experience from inside the other's framework. Today we are less willing to label a group of strangers as our enemy. It is a moving example of a culture evolving in empathic awareness.

Practice 90

THE ENEMY IN WAR

Some of you are soldiers and veterans; some of you are peace activists and veterans; some of you lost someone you loved in a war; and some of you lived through war in your home country before coming to this country. In your mind you will need to create the setting of war that makes the most sense to you. Begin by letting a group, country or cultural identification define who you are. Then we will expand the boundaries.

Put yourself into your group, your position. You are on one side of a boundary.

Face your enemy. In the culture of war, the enemy is often faceless. Let any images of the enemy float through your mind. Let whatever happens, happen. Whether the images represent a group or a person or both, just let them come to you.

Now, look at your own side. Allow images of your group to float through your mind. Let actual memories and imagined scenes come to you. Do you feel anger? Do you feel fear? Do you feel the excitement of preparing for a fight, of being part of a great cause, of winning a battle? Let yourself feel whatever emotions the images bring to you.

Return to the images of your enemy. What are they feeling? Try to sense their emotions. Let the boundary between yourself and the enemy start to dissolve in the connection you find at an emotional level. We are all young men and women, we are all mothers and fathers, we are all innocent children. We are all afraid of dying in a violent way. The war itself connects us.

Head a page of your journal "The Enemy in War." Write about your thoughts and feelings during this practice. Did you sense empathically the feelings of the enemy? Did you feel compassion for the suffering of the other? Does it lead you to want to take action?

A PERSONAL ENEMY

If we could read the secret history of our enemies, we would find in each man's life a sorrow and a suffering enough to disarm all hostility.

HENRY WADSWORTH LONGFELLOW

I don't have any personal history. One day I found out that personal history was no longer necessary for me and, like drinking, I dropped it.

CARLOS CASTANEDA

We are going to look now at a situation in which someone you know personally has hurt you. It may have happened once or many times. It may be someone with whom you work. It may be someone with whom you were once very close, a friend. In thinking about this situation, it is best not to choose a relative. Focus on someone who is outside the boundaries of the family, and has hurt you so much that you call him or her the enemy.

In the forest, in order to eat, animals hunt and kill. If someone moves to harm her cubs, a mother bear will attack and kill. These are natural, necessary survival actions. Certain emotions, such as anger, may be just as necessary psychologically for us as humans. In the following practices, you must tune into yourself, and sense if your anger is necessary for you now, at this moment. If you were deeply hurt and that anger is essential for you, then do not let anyone, even yourself, talk you into losing it. You will know when, if ever, it is time to stop being angry. And only you can know. For the practices involving a personal enemy, choose a relationship that you sense, through your empathic self-awareness, you want to change in some way.

Practice 91

WHAT A PERSONAL ENEMY MEANS TO ME

Think about why someone becomes a personal enemy to you. You can include acts of the person, such as hurting you with no justification, and feelings of your own, such as strong anger. What makes someone an enemy?

Head a page of your journal "What an Enemy Means to Me." Then list, in any order and however they come to you, the things that make someone an enemy for you. Write down whatever you think of when you think of an enemy.

Practice 92

A PERSONAL ENEMY

Choose one person and think about the story of your relationship, what that person did and how he became your enemy. *Let yourself feel the emotions that occur when you relive this story. These emotions are strong, and they are part of you. If this person is an enemy, you probably feel anger, even rage, and certainly pain. Remember that compassion for another is intertwined with compassion for yourself. Stay open to your own feelings.*

Now, think back again to one of the scenes in which you were hurt by this person. If you can, let part of yourself hover over the scene, looking down upon the person and yourself. Or, you might find it easier to imagine yourself and the person on a theater stage, acting out your roles in the story. The other part of you is watching the play from above.

Head a page of your journal "What I Am Feeling in the Scene Between Me and My Enemy." Write down the thoughts and feelings of you as the actor. Stay within the structure of the scene—you in that situation at that time in relation to that person. This is important because you might have felt differently about a slightly different situation, or the same situation at a different time in your life, or with another person. Describe the details of the scene as concretely as possible.

Look down again at the scene between you and your enemy. Now, using all of your empathic abilities, sense what your enemy is feeling. Let the boundary between the two of you dissolve for a moment, and get inside the other person's framework. Be in his situation, in his body. See the room or the scene through his eyes. Feel the tension through his body. Pick up whatever your enemy is feeling.

Head a page of your journal "What My Enemy Is Feeling in the Scene." Describe the situation from the other person's framework. Be as specific as you can about details: the room, the view, and of course, the feelings. What was the other person feeling in the scene? Were you able to put yourself in his framework? Did it make the other person feel less like an enemy?

Practice 93

GOING TO THE OTHER PERSON

Do this only if it feels right to you. If, in the last practice, you found that putting yourself in the other person's place changed your experience, then you may want to actually go to this person. You can do this in any way that makes sense in the context of the relationship. If the person feels less like an enemy now, you may want to say that. If it feels right to you, you can change the nature of the relationship between you.

EMPATHY FOR A STRANGER: THE PERCEPTION OF DANGER

> *We want our minds to be clear—not so we can think clearly, but so we can be open in our perceptions.*
>
> M. C. RICHARDS

> *Tell me to what you pay attention and I will tell you who you are.*
>
> JOSE ORTEGA Y GASSET

We meet a person unexpectedly, with few preconceptions. We are unaware, at the time of the meeting, that there is a real and important empathic connection between us. This situation is extremely interesting, because it has probably happened to all of us, even many times, yet many of us are unaware of it. In this sense it is very different from the other experiences in this chapter.

A woman closed her office door on the twelfth floor of the building and walked down the empty hall. The elevators were at the end, two of them. She pushed the down button and it lit up. She waited. Then a man stepped beside her. His presence was startling because she hadn't seen anyone in the hall and thought that the other offices were all closed for the night. But, she thought, an office could have been open further down the hall. He could have been delivering something to one of the offices. Yet she remained uneasy.

The elevator did not come. They waited together. Her sense that something was wrong increased as she waited with him. She sensed that he was nervous or upset. She told herself that it could be the nervousness people who are in a rush always feel when made to wait for elevators. It did not necessarily have anything to do with her. Yet she felt connected somehow to his tension. She felt that he was highly aware of her, even though his eyes were focused elsewhere. And she was aware of him.

Her mind was concentrating on the elevator, on its arrival. She felt that when it came the tension would be over. It finally rumbled to a stop and the doors opened. It was empty.

For some reason she had not thought of this possibility. A wave of fear flowed through her. The man did not move. But again, there was a rational explanation: men often wait for women to get onto the elevator first. All of this thinking and sensing took place in a few seconds. She was afraid to step into the elevator alone with him. If she stayed on the floor, she could run back to her office where a friend was still working, and if the man grabbed her, she could at least scream and hope that her friend would hear. In the elevator there would be no escape.

Yet she stepped into the elevator. The man followed, the doors closed, and he raped her.

Many people who have been attacked have sensed beforehand that they were in danger. They sensed that there was something to fear *before* they entered an elevator or an empty place, but they did not act on their instincts.

If someone is about to harm you, that person is feeling intense emotions. It doesn't matter whether these emotions are nervousness, fear, hate, or any combination of these. The important thing is that the person is feeling something intensely, and this intensity can be picked up. If the emotion is directed toward you, it is even more likely that you would sense something. You do not necessarily pick up a specific emotion; you just sense a disturbance; something is wrong. The woman at the elevator sensed, correctly, that something was wrong and that it was connected to her.

If empathy is a perceptual ability, then like our other perceptual systems it has survival value. It provides information about the world around us, and as part of that function it warns of the presence of danger. It can be a highly developed, conscious ability in people whose lives are constantly exposed to danger: police officers, soldiers in combat, those who live with someone who is physically abusive. Part of developing our empathic ability is developing this special aspect: our sense of danger. As with all cases of empathy, it involves increasing our awareness and our ability to trust. In this case, however, it means trusting ourselves.

Practice 94

EMPATHY FOR STRANGERS

You can do this practice whenever you are in a public place with strangers. Supermarkets and restaurants are interesting and normally safe places to observe people.

Pick one person and watch for a while. Of course you cannot stare at that person. Even if you watch unobtrusively, using peripheral vision, you may find that the person notices you and becomes uncomfortable. He or she is being empathic, picking up a sense of your presence and an uncomfortable feeling of connection.

Some people, however, will not notice you. And in some situations, such as waiting in line at the cash register, you can be aware without actually looking. Try to sense anything you can about the other person. Just let any insights come to you. See if you can pick up a general sense of their presence. What are they paying attention to? Are they aware of you? Are they focused on their own actions? Are they drifting someplace in their own world?

Repeat this practice whenever you feel like it. If you ever sense danger, trust your feelings. Act from your knowledge that there is a real connection between people, even strangers, and that sometimes this connection can warn you that something is wrong.

In the next chapter we will look at our connections to the natural world, and the rhythms of nature within and around us.

12 COMPASSION AND EMPATHY FOR THE NATURAL WORLD

*The most difficult part about the warrior's way is to realize that
the world is a feeling.*

CARLOS CASTANEDA

*My words are tied in one
With the great mountains,
With the great rocks,
With the great trees,
In one with my body
And my heart.*
TEWA INDIAN CHANT

HAVE YOU WATCHED A horse fall, breaking its leg and trying
to get up, and felt inside you the suffering? Have you felt this
kind of connection with a wounded bird? With a tree? With
the earth where it has been dug into, leaving huge holes?

Ask yourself if you can draw a line. Can you feel compassion for a human being and not for the earth and sky?

In many spiritual traditions there is an unbroken connection between all things in the natural world. When we looked
earlier at the connection between adults and children, we
spoke of the sacredness of trust. A similar sacredness of respect occurs at the center of other cultures, and in some way in
our own culture, between humans and the natural world.

Respect is shown in many different ways. A native hunter
talks to the animal he has just killed, thanking it for providing
food. A shaman talks to a plant before picking it. Some people

are vegetarians because they are not willing to kill animals. Some cultures do not build temples; they celebrate their spirituality in their connection with the natural world.

In the sacredness of respect, you perceive the connectedness of all things. In some cultures, it is said that you *see* the world differently. In other cultures, the connection is described as an insight, an inner seeing. But in all cultures, when you feel this connection, you do not feel superior or controlling or cruel toward anything. It does not mean you will act in any specific way. Compassion is not a way of judging others or judging yourself. It is a connection that includes hunters and mountain lions, fishermen and trout. The sacredness of respect is an inner feeling about the world. It is a sense of connection between yourself and another living creature, between your life and the life of the oceans. With this sense of connection, actions do change. These changes come from your center, from a deepening awareness of your own respect for the natural world.

EMPATHY FOR ANIMALS

> *Animals teach us about the animal in ourselves. We need their spirits.*
>
> MATTHEW FOX

> *One does not meet oneself until one catches the reflection from an eye other than human.*
>
> LOREN EISELEY

I have learned a great deal about the rhythms of empathy from my dogs. I may think about a rhythm in some sophisticated way that would never occur to my dog. Dogs and infants do not think the way we do. But they pick up the world's rhythms and respond rhythmically to the world. With an animal you are totally immersed in the bodily, nonverbal level of communication.

Practice 95

THREE BASIC RHYTHMS

This practice is especially useful for those of you who live with an animal. You can try parts of it with any animal. But if you do not know the animal, respect its instincts and power, which may include fear of you, and the ability to attack. Empathy is not some sentimental assumption that nature is harmless and nonviolent. Empathy is perceiving the living rhythms that are there.

Begin by observing three basic rhythms of the animal: excitement, calm, and focused alertness. Observe the times when these rhythms occur most clearly. With my dog, for example, excitement is clearest when I have left him alone for a while and then I come home.

When you have identified a characteristic time for each of the rhythms, focus your attention completely upon the animal during these times. Watch, listen, and feel whatever comes to you. Try to sense in your own body what the animal is feeling.

Head a page of your journal "Three Basic Rhythms." Describe each rhythm: excitement, calm, and focused alertness. Did you learn anything about the rhythm by tuning into the animal?

Practice 96

MY ANIMAL'S RESPONSE TO ME

Play with the animal, communicating the three basic rhythms of excitement, calm, and focused attention. See how the animal responds. See if the animal echoes your rhythms.

Head a page of your journal "My Animal's Response to Me." Describe your experiences with your animal, your communication of excitement, calm, and focused alertness, and the animal's response to you. How did you communicate each rhythm? Did the animal echo the rhythm? Did you sense an empathic connection between you? At moments, would you describe the connection as mutual empathy?

You can trick an animal, by hopping around and waving your arms in the air, into picking up the sense of excitement. And it could also be the case that, if your heart is racing with fear, but you are putting on a show of external calm, you will not be able to fool the animal. The perception of a rhythm such as excitement or calm is based upon a combination of things. An animal and a human might focus on one thing, such as your arms waving around, and miss other things. The purpose of these practices is not to separate the various elements involved in awareness, but to increase awareness of the rhythms as a whole.

COMPASSION FOR ANIMALS

> They covered the [stranded] whales with mud to keep them cool and protect them from the sun, sprinkled them with water, stroked them and tried to comfort them.
>
> JUDITH GAINES

Anything you do matters. There is so much cruelty in our world, it is difficult to know where to start or how far to go. How you approach this depends upon your feelings and your situation at this time. If you work on your own awareness, things will happen.

Practice 97

COMPASSION FOR AN ANIMAL

For this practice, do one thing that is an act of compassion for an animal. Choose an act that is new for you, something you have not regularly been doing. If you find a spider in your house, you could carefully carry it outside instead of killing it. If you have been neglecting your dog,

*play with it and comfort it. If you are moved to do this and
are able, help save the life of some wild animal that lives in
your environment.*

*Head a page of your journal "Compassion for an Ani-
mal." Write about what you did, and your feelings about
it. Describe the sense of connection between the animal
and you.*

EMPATHY FOR THE ENVIRONMENT

If something is alive, those who are also alive will resonate with it.
RAIMON PANIKKAR

*The seashore is the frontier between two realms. It is a disputed
zone between the sea and the land, where the fortunes of each
side ebb and flow with the tides.*
ROBERT BURTON

Each of us, at this moment, is connected to our environment. It is only a question of awareness. Take a deep breath
and feel the surrounding air enter and leave your body. You and
the air share a moving boundary. You have a steady, rhythmic
connection with the air around you.

As you move through the world, you move in relation to air,
earth, and water. Imagine a fish swimming in a pool. As the
fish moves it parts the water, creating small rhythms. The
rhythm of the water influences the fish's motion. Whatever is
part of the water affects the life and death of the fish. In the
next few practices, you will look at your own connection to the
substance of your world.

Practice 98

THE AIR AROUND ME

*Go to a natural setting where you feel comfortable and
free. Focus on your breath as you take in air and return it
to the surrounding space. What is the air like today? Is it*

cold and crisp or warm and soft? Is there a strong wind, a light breeze, or stillness? Feel the air on your skin. Feel it flow inside your body and out again as you breathe.

Practice 99

THE SUPPORTING GROUND

Go to a natural setting where you feel safe and take off your shoes. Walk barefoot, focusing on the feeling of the ground touching your feet. Do this on different kinds of ground: the sand of a beach, the grasses of a field, the rocks of a stream. Feel the connection between the way you walk and the ground beneath you. Sense the rhythm of your walk changing as the substance of the ground changes. Feel the way the ground supports you. You and the ground share a moving boundary. The sand indents, changing its shape, at the pressure of your foot. Your foot gives to the pressure of the rock.

Practice 100

WATER

Go into the water and focus completely on the water's rhythm. Float with the water's motion. Swim slowly and feel the rhythmic interaction between your motions and the pull of the water. Compare the interaction in choppy and calm water, in a river, a pond, or the ocean.

If it is winter now, do this practice with ice and snow. Skate over the ice and feel the relation between your gliding motion and the smooth surface. Ski or walk in deep snow and let yourself feel the connection between your motions and the substance of your world.

Head a page of your journal "My Connection to Air, Earth and Water." Describe your bodily sensations, and your feelings, in the three practices above. Were you aware *of the boundaries between you and the air, the ground, and the water? Did you feel the movement of these boundaries, the rhythm of the changes between you? Did you feel connected to your surrounding world?*

THE PERCEPTION OF RHYTHMIC STRUCTURE

> *Any good hitter can tell you the feeling. The ball is coming up to the plate and it seems like everything is in slow motion.*
>
> ROD CAREW

We perceive the world in terms of rhythmic structures. Our bodies are tuned to pick up changes—from motion to stillness, from light to dark—and the stable repetition of these changes over time. Our bodies have their own rhythmic structures: the beating of our heart, the rise and fall of our breath, the patterns of brain waves. And the world around us creates a constant stream of rhythmic structures. Visually, we watch the rhythm of different motions: someone moving slowly, someone moving quickly, someone moving toward or away from us, trees blowing in the wind, and ocean waves rolling in and drawing back. Sound also is a stream of patterns flowing around and through us. We listen to the sound of the wind, of the human voice, of animals moving across the ground. Our minds are designed to pick up rhythmic structures.

Practice 101

THE RHYTHM OF A NATURAL EVENT

For this practice, focus for some time on a natural event in which there is motion. You can go to a stream or the ocean and watch the water. You don't have to be outside. Many people love watching a storm from their window. From the calm of your room, you can watch the trees swaying or the clouds floating by on a windy day.

The purpose of this practice is to tune into the rhythm of the natural event. Let yourself feel the energy inside you. Become aware of the rhythm of the event. This rhythm may remind you of a human emotion. You can sometimes experience a storm as angry; sometimes you can feel it as pure power. You can feel the great energy of a storm inside you with or without giving it human qualities; this is an individual matter. Either way, when you feel the rhythm of a natural event inside you, you are experiencing nature empathically.

Head a page of your journal "The Rhythm of a Natural Event." Describe the rhythm, and your own response. Did you feel excited or calmed by the rhythm? Did you sense a human emotion in the rhythm? Did you feel an empathic connection to the natural event?

COMPASSION FOR THE ENVIRONMENT

I shall never forget the nights under the Saharan stars. I felt as if I were wrapped around by the blanket of the friendly night, a blanket embroidered by the stars.

CARLO CARRETTO

Violence is intrinsic to the universe. Terror and beauty go together.

MATTHEW FOX

Ultimately, the decision to save the environment must come from the human heart.

THE DALAI LAMA

As we become aware of our connection to the natural world, compassion follows. We have talked about the basis of universal compassion: we are connected to each other, so that when one of us suffers, we each feel that suffering. The same understanding leads us to compassion for the environment. We are connected to the earth and the sky. When they are harmed, we are harmed.

By harming the environment, I mean disrupting the natural cycles of growth and decay. The destructive force could itself be natural, a hurricane or an earthquake. The natural world is vulnerable to itself just as we are vulnerable. It is this vulnerability that creates the possibility of compassion. But so often today, the destructive force is of human origin: oil spills, toxic waste, devastation of forests. Compassion for the environment means feeling the destruction of the earth as a hurt inside you.

Compassion includes the desire to help in some way. After natural disasters we help to restore the land. And we do this work of restoration after human disasters. We try to clean our beaches after oil spills.

But the essence of compassion for the environment resides in what Ram Dass said: "Compassion is not interfering." People who are deeply involved in their connection to the environment teach us, essentially, to not interfere. It is human interference that has polluted the air and water, dumped toxic wastes into the ocean, cut down forests and gouged out the earth.

Noninterference returns us to the sacredness of respect: respect for the rhythm of flowing water, respect for the cycles of growth and decay, life and death, of the natural world. It is our world, and we are *inside* it. It is inside us. We are connected. Let yourself be easy and clear about that connection.

Practice 102

COMPASSION FOR THE ENVIRONMENT

Do one thing for the environment that is new for you, and which fits your feeling of how you want to help. You have to feel the connection yourself. Think about what you would really like to do, and then do it.

Head a page of your journal "Compassion for the Environment." Describe what you chose to do and your feelings about it. Did you feel respect?

AN IMAGE OF THE EARTH

> *Truth is ever found in simplicity, and not in the multiplicity and confusion of things.*
>
> ISAAC NEWTON

> *For tribal cultures, Earth is seen as a whole and living organism.*
>
> JOAN HALIFAX

When I was a child, we memorized the planets in their order from the sun: Mercury, Venus, Earth, Mars, Jupiter, Saturn, Uranus, Neptune, and Pluto. We had an image of the planets as little balls revolving mechanically, something like a mobile. It was only in imagination—Milton describing the way the earth looks from heaven; comic book artists showing the earth from outer space—that we had an image of a whole, living earth.

Today, we have incredible photographs of our planet taken from space. And we have astronauts who have seen the earth as a single image, a whole, and have said that it was a spiritual experience. We have an image of the wholeness of the earth.

Mary Watkins said that to have world peace, we need to be able to visualize it. We have many images of war and violence. We need images of peace.

Because we now have an image of our planet, when scientists say that pollution in one part of the world spreads to all of the world, their words are real. We can picture the atmosphere circling the earth. We can see that this atmosphere encircling the earth touches everything on the earth. It is *our* atmosphere.

We are evolving, as a culture, in our awareness of the connectedness of the earth. In seeking awareness, many people have studied traditions in which the natural world has always been seen as a whole, and each being is inseparable from this whole. Buddhism is one of these traditions. Peter Levitt writes: "There is a teaching in Buddhist tradition which tells us that each atom in the universe, at one time or another, has been our mother. And that we have been the mother of each atom as well. . . . To grasp even a little of this teaching makes quite a difference in how we move through the world." We begin to move through the world with an awareness of the air and the water that is like our awareness of another person. We begin to move through the world with the sense of being connected.

Practice 103

AN IMAGE OF THE EARTH

In this practice, you can create an image of the earth as a whole. Imagine yourself outside, in some natural setting. Now imagine that you are going into the air. You can imagine being in an airplane, in a spaceship, or flying by yourself. Watch the houses and cars getting smaller and smaller. See the water and land forming patterns as you view them from the distance. Keep climbing until you are out there in space. See the earth as one single image, a living sphere.

Head a page of your journal "An Image of the Earth." Describe the things that you saw. How did you feel?

THE BOUNDARIES OF THE EARTH

Dwelling in harmony means dwelling as if life in the broadest sense, not just human life, really matters.

BILL DEVALL

We take this long journey, separating things and trying to understand them; then we come back to where we started, to the notion of primal unity, and the sacred and mysterious quality of this process that we are all engaged in.

BRIAN GOODWIN

All . . . would flow naturally and easily if the self were widened and deepened so that the protection of nature was felt and perceived as protection of our very selves.

ARNE NAESS

We have spoken of empathic connections as dissolving the ordinary boundaries between people. In empathy, we are connected to each other's inner worlds.

If we think of empathy as the perception of rhythmic structure, we experience the natural world empathically. We have looked at the rhythms of the wind and flowing water as a kind of empathy. When we are tuned to the natural world in this way, the ordinary boundaries between ourselves and the world dissolve.

There is a way of expressing this interdependence of the self and the world called: *deep ecology*. In deep ecology, the natural world is understood as a living, coherent system. Like the human body, it is a system that responds to change. When it is out of balance, it tries to bring the various forces back into balance. When it is wounded, it works to heal itself.

When something is understood as a system, elements which were previously considered separately are now seen as influencing and depending upon each other. The human body is an example. Until recently, western science looked at the brain and the immune system as separate systems. Within this scientific framework, it was impossible for something happening in the mind to affect something happening in the immune system. It was not understood how a mental event, such as loneliness, could decrease the effectiveness of the immune system. It was not understood how a sense of inner peace, or a feeling of hope, could strengthen the immune system.

Scientists are now able to conceive of the human body as one unified system. They have found, as a very real possibility, that the brain and the immune system communicate with each other. The brain receives messages from the immune system about the presence of a virus, and the immune system receives messages from the brain about the presence of feelings. The different elements in the system are in touch with each other. The condition of one affects the condition of the other. This understanding of interdependence was possible only when two smaller systems were approached as a single system. Our scientific culture needed an image of the human body as a whole.

Deep ecology is an understanding of the earth, the planet on which we live, as one unified system. We, as human beings, are one of the elements in the larger system. As Peter Levitt said, when we begin to grasp even a little of this way of thinking, our way of experiencing things changes. We begin to see our human condition as dependent upon the condition of the earth. We begin to see the condition of the earth as dependent upon the condition of our inner world. We are one system *within* another system.

In the practice of compassion, we have experienced the fluidity of boundaries. When we feel compassion for another person, we feel deeply connected to that person. At the level of feelings, the boundary between us is gone.

Deep ecology expresses the same fluidity of boundaries between the earth and ourselves. We are held and protected by that larger system, the earth. When we protect the earth, we are protecting all of the systems within the earth, including ourselves. We can actually experience the boundaries of the self expanding to include the earth.

Practice 104

The Boundaries of the Earth

Imagine the earth in a single image. You are hovering someplace in space, and you see the earth below you, as a living, unified sphere.

Now, imagine that you see that the earth is damaged in some way. You might see the pollution in the atmosphere. You can see the clouds and the air currents swirling around, carrying the pollution across the globe. A tree in your backyard is fed by raindrops collected in the atmosphere that encircles the world.

Look down at the earth. Think about the damaged earth. Think about the earth as needing protection.

Head a page of your journal "The Boundaries of the Earth." Describe what you saw. What were your feelings?

Did you feel, in any way, that you wanted to protect the earth? Did you feel, in some sense, as if the earth was part of you?

The sacredness of respect leads us gently into the spiritual world, and the sense of spiritual connection. We will look at this sense of connection in the final chapter, the way of compassion and empathy.

13 THE WAY OF COMPASSION AND EMPATHY

The whole idea of compassion is based on a keen awareness of the interdependence of all these living beings, which are all part of one another and all involved in one another.

THOMAS MERTON

Through the discipline of prayer we awaken ourselves to the God in us and let him enter into our heartbeat and our breathing, into our thoughts and emotions, our hearing, seeing, touching, and tasting.

HENRI NOUWEN

You cannot know it, but you can be it At ease in your own life.

LAO TZU

*F*OR MANY YEARS I wondered what people meant by a way, as in "The way of the Tao." A *way,* in one of its meanings, is a path on a spiritual journey. In this sense, the path of compassion is one part of a greater journey to spiritual awareness.

Another meaning of a *way* is a discipline. In spiritual communities, disciplines such as prayer and meditation are passed on from teacher to student. In other communities, certain kinds of knowledge—how to watch the ball, how to plant corn—are passed on. A discipline involves the conscious practice of some kind of knowledge. Being on a *way* means staying with the practice, working through fears and blocks, to reach awareness.

Finally, a *way* can be simply how you are in your life, your way of being. In this sense, you can live the way of empathy and compassion without thinking of it as either a path or a discipline. This book has approached empathy as a perceptual ability, like the sense of touch. If this is correct, then all of us are empathic, although fears and cultural ideas can block our awareness of our own nature. When we have that awareness, we are there: that is our way.

These three meanings of a *way* are really three approaches to awareness. You can decide which approach, or combination of approaches, feels right to you. The approaches are closely related, and you may find that all three are important to you. Listen to your feelings and trust yourself. Ask yourself if you feel at home with the emphasis of the approach.

Feeling at home is an inner feeling that may have no clear connection to your external life. Recently I drove my son to the train station, in a town where I have worked for many years. As we waited on the platform, I looked around and had the feeling that I had dropped down from the sky into an unknown land. Yet I have been to places I had never seen before, an island off the coast of Japan, a market in Budapest, where I felt at home.

You also can ask yourself, now, if you feel at home with the way of empathy and compassion in general, regardless of the approach. If you feel at home with this way, the basic concepts of this book have probably seemed familiar to you. They found a resonating echo inside you. You have probably been living the way of empathy and compassion, without necessarily using these, or any, words. Or, perhaps you have been preparing for this way, gathering awareness. In the next practice, you can think about how you want to continue on this way.

Practice 105

CONTINUING ON THE WAY

For this practice, consider the three meanings of a way, *as part of a spiritual path, as a discipline, and as a natural way of perceiving the world. First, ask yourself how you have approached empathy and compassion up until now.*

Next, ask which approach, or combination of approaches, feels right for you now. Do you want to be on a spiritual path? Do you want to work, with concentration and commitment, on compassion as a discipline? Do you want to let awareness happen in the process of living your daily life?

Many people follow the three approaches together. It helps, however, to see which approach most clearly draws you. It helps, for example, to see that a discipline is something you long for, something you want to begin; or, alternatively, to see that a discipline is not the right approach for you, that you need, at this point in your life, to let yourself be.

Head a page of your journal "Continuing on the Way." Describe how the three approaches have fit into your life until now. Then write down your thoughts and feelings about how you want each approach to be part of your life right now.

COMPASSION AND EMPATHY AS EXPERIENCES OF SPIRITUAL UNION

The core of Judaism is the irrepressible hunch that the unity of all beings is beyond all physical representation.

RABBI HAROLD KUSHNER

. . . This touch which is not of the senses, which is not of the intellect, but is substantial.

ST. JOHN OF THE CROSS

A sense of union takes us out of our ordinary way of experiencing and brings us into another realm. We can experience this connection in many ways. One description of this experience is that we feel whole. This wholeness is essentially a spiritual feeling. It is a sense of being connected in a transcendent way. With this feeling we enter the spiritual world.

SPIRITUAL EMPATHY

> *We couldn't talk much. We looked at each other's face. I got a*
> *very happy experience, some kind of vibration.*
>   The Dalai Lama (on meeting a Christian monk)

You have experienced empathy as a feeling of union in many of the practices. If your friend is feeling happy, and you are open to the feeling, you feel the happiness inside you. This is already a profound connection. Now your friend picks up your response, and feels peaceful and content in the happiness between you. Nothing has to be hidden, there is no fear, no need to defend the self. Your friend's happiness deepens in this connection with you. You are united in the echoing feeling.

Our experience of empathy can give us a glimpse of a spiritual world. In this world, in openness and freedom, we can be unified with everything. Our connection brings a sense of great peace, within and around us. The normal sense of boundaries is not there.

We each come to spiritual awareness in our own way. We have different personal qualities; we tune in more naturally to different modes of communication, and we relate more easily to different spiritual traditions. In the next practice, you can imagine spiritual empathy in your own way.

Practice 106

Spiritual Empathy

Recall an experience of connection in which you felt trans-ported to another world by the strength and beauty of the connection. You may have felt an unusual energy, perhaps a radiance, that was both around and within you. You may have felt a perfect calm around you, and within you an in-ner peace.

Relive the experience. Let yourself feel the nature of the union.

Head a page of your journal "Spiritual Empathy." De-scribe the details of the experience and the feeling of union.

COMPASSION AS SPIRITUAL UNION

Surely he hath bourne our griefs,
And carried our sorrows.

ISAIAH

The hearing of his name, the sight of his body,
And the recollection of him in thought do not pass away
    in vain,
For he can extinguish the woes of existence.

BUDDHA (THE LOTUS SUTRA)

When he saw the crowds, he had compassion for them, because
they were harassed and helpless, like sheep without a shepherd.

MATTHEW

We have spoken of compassion as feeling the suffering of another person and acting in some way. But we also spoke of the times, which unfortunately seem to be many, in which we cannot act. There is still, however, the desire to act. It is that feeling of wanting to relieve the suffering, of wanting to save another person, that pulls us to action.

Let us look at action for a moment. Remember the example in chapter 5 of the mother who empathically sensed her child's fear? She felt the fear, sensed the danger, and acted to save the child's life. When we sense someone in danger, especially our child, we are pulled to act. Yet this is not what we mean by compassion.

Compassion seems inextricably connected to the feeling of suffering. When you rush to pull a drowning child out of the water, you are not feeling suffering. You are feeling fear or sensing danger. It is a life or death situation and you act as quickly as possible. At the moment of action you are probably not aware of feeling anything—you are totally concentrated in the action itself.

Compassion is different. In compassion you feel the suffering and you feel, almost overwhelmingly, the desire to help. You feel a connection to the other person that makes you want to take on their suffering. You want to hold them, or reach them in some way, so that their suffering will end.

This powerful feeling of connection seems to be central in the teachings of both Jesus and the Buddha. The details are quite different, but the feeling of their compassion seems the same.

Practice 107

COMPASSION AS SPIRITUAL UNION

Recall an experience of compassion in which you felt compelled to take on the other person's suffering. Relive the experience. Let yourself feel as deeply as possible that desire to heal the suffering. How would you describe the nature of that feeling? Would you describe it as union, as love?

Head a page of your journal "Compassion: The Feeling of Spiritual Union." Describe the feeling of wanting to take on the suffering. Was there a spiritual aspect to the feeling?

This chapter is a chance to reflect upon the role of empathy and compassion in the next part of your life. You may want to create an image of the future. There are two very different possibilities to consider. The first possibility is active, purposeful helping—the path of compassion. It is going out and being in the world. The other is, in some ways, the opposite—solitude. You will find that one depends upon the other. If you stay with the practice of compassion and empathy, you can count on both in your life.

THE PATH OF COMPASSION

> *They shall not hurt nor destroy*
> *In all my holy mountain.*
>   ISAIAH

All of Buddha's teachings can be expressed in two sentences . . . "You must help others. If not, you should not harm others."

THE DALAI LAMA

The enlightened ones are loving and compassionate, and the mystical experience is frequently described as one of deep solidarity with all mankind.

CLAUDIO NARANJO

When we look at people who are suffering from poverty and illness in our own country, we sometimes make assumptions: they could get a job, or get medical care, if they tried. We give advice, actually or silently in our minds. But when we are traveling in a foreign country, we know that we do not know. We find ourselves in a strange framework. We look around and try to *see.*

Traveling to a strange country is like the inner journey to a different reality. In a strange framework we need to give attention to things that we normally take for granted. The movement of the people, their daily routines of eating, working, and sleeping, are unfamiliar in many details. People may be eating their food with chopsticks or their fingers. They may bathe in a public bath or beside a stream. In this new framework, we suddenly become aware of the shape of the food and the touch of the water.

If we do not know the language, we give all our attention to the nonverbal modes of communicating: the look on the other person's face, the focus of her eyes, the hand motions, the tone of voice. We tune into feelings, using our empathic ability more fully.

Perhaps this is why, in a foreign country, we feel compassion more clearly. We are tuned into the present moment. We are tuned to the realm of feelings. Open to feelings, we sense the reality of suffering and echo that feeling.

Traveling frees us to be aware. But we can be aware in our own cities and forests. There are many guides to active compassion and the helping of others. This book has focused on compassion in personal relationships. But the circle of compassion, which might start with two people, naturally widens. We come to the insight that we are all connected.

Practice 108

THE PATH OF COMPASSION

For this practice, decide where you want to go and how you want to help. Think about the right place and go there. Look around you as if you were in a strange country. Try not to make any assumptions—about the culture, the people, anything. Try to be there, in that place at that moment, with all your awareness.

Then, if there is a way to do something which comes from your inner feeling of connection, do something to help.

SOLITUDE

I asked him: "What did you practice during your years of solitude?" "I concentrated on love," he told me.

THE DALAI LAMA
(IN CONVERSATION WITH A CHRISTIAN MONK)

Solitude is essential for community life because there we begin to discover a unity that is prior to all unifying action.

HENRI NOUWEN

Solitude is being with your self. In the practices of imagination and reflection, and in your journal writing, you have been working alone. You have done much inner work in solitude.

Solitude is the other side of the path of compassion. People who have committed their lives to helping others speak of the importance of being alone, of being at peace with themselves. In solitude we find the awareness that enables us to be aware of others. In solitude we face our own vulnerability so that we can accept the vulnerability of others.

The communication of self and spirit comes most naturally when we are alone. Of course, we are not really alone when we are with spiritual presence. We are simply without the presence of other people. Henri Nouwen says that in solitude we find the essential unity that makes possible all unifying actions. Our unifying actions, our acts of compassion, are grounded in our sense of the unity of all things.

Practice 109

SPACES OF SOLITUDE

For this practice, think of places where you feel comfortable being alone. Think of situations in which you feel best when you are alone. We each have places and situations where we can be alone and feel especially open and free. It might be the special space of a cathedral, or the great expanse of ocean and sky. It might be in your own room. Imagine your own spaces.

Head a page of your journal "Spaces of Solitude." Describe the spaces in which you feel most comfortable, most your self, being alone.

Go to one of your spaces of solitude. Try going to that place when you feel upset in some way. When you need to be quiet inside your self, to get in touch with your self, go to that space. See if that space can become a sanctuary for you.

Practice 110

A PLAN FOR THE FUTURE

Close your eyes, take a deep breath, and let yourself breathe quietly. Relax. Let images of empathy and compassion flow through your mind. In doing the practices and reflecting upon your experiences, you have collected many images. Let these images, or any new ones, float in and out of your mind.

Now, think about what you would like to create in the future. This image could be anything related to empathy and compassion. It could be that you will go and talk to one of your parents. It could be that you will spend more time in solitude, increasing your awareness. It could be that you will become involved in some form of active compassion. Your plan is whatever you decide will be the next step in your life. Try to let it come to you as an image, a vision for you. Don't force yourself to construct it. If no image comes to you, be patient. Be there with yourself in the moment, whatever is happening.

Head a page of your journal "A Plan for the Future." Write about your image of the future.

Think about the three approaches to being on a way: as a spiritual path, as a discipline, and as a part of your daily life. In your journal entry for Practice 105, how did you think that each of these approaches would fit into your life? Now, think about your plan. Do the approaches and your plan make sense together? Do you see how the approaches will help you to realize your plan? In your journal entry above, add your thoughts about how the approaches will help you to realize your plan.

AN EMPATHIC BEING IN CHILDHOOD

> *What I mean by the mystical is the capability of immediate contemplation of the real.*
>
> RAIMUNDO PANIKKAR

> *If you descend into the depths of your own spirit . . . and arrive somewhere near the center of what you are, you are confronted with the inescapable truth that, at the root of your existence, you are in constant and immediate contact with the infinite power of God.*
>
> THOMAS MERTON

You may remember having an imaginary friend when you were a child. Perhaps you communicated with an animal or a spiritual being. You may have identified so closely with a comic book character that you experienced that character's inner world. Frequently, these characters have special abilities—seeing through walls or seeing into other people's minds—that cross through the boundaries of the ordinary world. Today, on "Star Trek: The Next Generation," children have Deanna Troi, an Empath, who perceives feelings in others. When we were children, my friends and I had Superman and Wonder Woman.

Empathy is so central to our inner being that we actively seek its presence in our lives. As children, we are more free to enter nonordinary worlds. We can explore empathic connections with anyone we want. We can find an empathic being in another world.

With our empathic being we can explore any feeling. We can explore feelings that no one in our ordinary world is capable of receiving. Our empathic being is open to any feeling. And we can accept and echo any feeling we discover in our empathic being. We can feel what it is like to fly, to see through walls, to read other people's minds. We can feel what it is like to be completely ourselves, completely at peace with another being. As a child, with intuitive wisdom, we practice empathy for ourselves. We find ourselves.

Practice 111

AN EMPATHIC BEING IN CHILDHOOD

Think of some being with whom you had a special connection as a child. It could be a spirit, an animal, a comic book character. Imagine the two of you together. How did you communicate? Were you feeling the same thing? Did you sense what that being was feeling without words? Relive the sense of communication between you.

*Head a page of your journal "My Empathic Being."
Write about your connection with the being. Do you think
that this empathic being has influenced the way you feel
about relationships now, as an adult?*

Practice 112

AN EMPATHIC BEING NOW

*In certain traditions, a person who is seeking insight finds
a teacher or guide for an inner journey. This guide is someone you encounter in your mind. The guide can come to
you in the form of a person, an animal, or some kind of
spiritual being.*

*For this practice, find an empathic being in the same
way a seeker finds a guide, a being in your inner world.*

*Your empathic being can be anyone or anything: it could
be that same being from childhood. It could be that you
will see, in your mind, a grandmother or grandfather who
is dead now. You might see a friend or an intimate companion. You might encounter a completely imaginary
being—that is, a being you have never met in any ordinary
way. You are seeking an empathic being for yourself now.*

*Close your eyes and think about significant, touchstone
experiences of empathy and compassion. Let images of
your experiences float through your mind.*

*After a few minutes, do you seem to be focusing on a
particular image? Does it keep returning? Does it seem
stronger than the others that drift through your mind? Is
that image an empathic being for you?*

*Head a page of your journal "An Empathic Being Now."
Who or what did you see? Did this being surprise you?
Write about your empathic being.*

Sometimes we surprise ourselves. We find deep connections with animals, imaginary characters, even bodies of water. Although we are significantly different from ourselves as
children, when we enter our minds, we can find the same
bonds of feeling.

A VISION OF FEELINGS

> *Therefore speak I to them in parables, because they seeing see not.*
>
> JESUS

> *Seeing . . . is the final accomplishment of a man of knowledge.*
> CARLOS CASTANEDA

The acceptance of different kinds of reality helps immensely in understanding the way of empathy and compassion. In the world of ordinary reality, feelings are subjective experiences. They cannot be communicated with any assurance of accuracy. Empathic connections remain in that murky zone of intuitions and insights that are not real and are hidden from awareness.

For a vision of feelings, we have to accept the reality of another world. It is a world of empathic connections and experiences of union. In this nonordinary world, we perceive feelings. We sense our connections to each other. In many spiritual traditions, it is said that we *see*. In the ordinary world we see colors and shapes which we identify as separate objects. In the spiritual world, we see the underlying unity of all things.

As adults, we can recapture that freedom we had as a child to seek and find empathic beings. We each find our own way of doing this. Some of us go back and forth between different worlds. We are there, present and aware, in our ordinary world. We are there, also, in an inner world, another reality. In that inner world we find the essential nature of empathy for us. And our nonordinary experiences of empathy change our awareness. We become tuned to the possibilities of empathy in the ordinary world. We begin to see other people in a different way. We have a vision of feelings.

This book began with a quotation from the Ashtravakra Gita, "Now I live in my heart." Living in your heart is feeling the unity of all things. It is the way of compassion and empathy. I hope that you will find your vision of feelings.